MW01711074

Test Bank

A Speaker's Guidebook

Test Bank

A Speaker's Guidebook

3rd edition

TEXT AND REFERENCE

Dan O'Hair
Rob Stewart
Hannah Rubenstein

Prepared by

Jennifer Emerling Bone
State University of New York, Oneonta

Merry Buchanan
Texas Christian University

BEDFORD / ST. MARTIN'S
Boston ♦ New York

Copyright © 2007 by Bedford/St. Martin's

All rights reserved.

Instructors who have adopted *A Speaker's Guidebook* as a textbook for a course are authorized to duplicate portions of this manual for their students.

Manufactured in the United States of America.

1 0 9 8 7
f e d c b a

For information, write: Bedford/St. Martin's, 75 Arlington Street, Boston, MA 02116 (617-399-4000)

ISBN-10: 0-312-45203-9
ISBN-13: 978-0-312-45203-2

PREFACE

The *Test Bank* to accompany *A Speaker's Guidebook,* 3rd edition, contains over 2,000 true/false, multiple-choice, fill-in-the-blank, short answer, and essay questions. The questions have been carefully crafted to test students' specific knowledge of the text. Also available is an *Electronic Test Bank* containing all of the test questions in a format that allows instructors to add their own questions and generate their own tests. The computerized version is available in Windows and Macintosh platforms. For more information on this ancillary, please call or write Bedford/St. Martin's, Faculty Services, 4B Cedarbrook Drive, Cranbury, NJ 08512 (866-843-3715), or contact your local Bedford/St. Martin's sales representative.

CONTENTS

Test Bank

A Speaker's Guidebook

Becoming a Public Speaker 1

TRUE/FALSE QUESTIONS

1. Learning to speak effectively can enhance your career as a student.
2. Communication skills top the list of job skills most employers seek.
3. A key feature of any type of communication is sensitivity to the listeners.
4. Public speaking can improve one's ability to reason and think critically.
5. Public speaking offers a very low level of feedback.
6. Unlike many forms of communication, public speaking usually occurs in formal settings.
7. The source is the person who receives the message.
8. The process of organizing the message, choosing words and sentence structures, and verbalizing the message is termed *encoding.*
9. The receiver decodes or interprets the message.
10. Audience members often selectively interpret the meaning of a speaker's message.
11. The audience's response to a message is called *audience perspective.*
12. The content of a message can be expressed both verbally and nonverbally.
13. Another term for noise is *interference.*
14. Noise is the medium through which a speaker sends a message.
15. The *channel* is the content of the communication process.
16. Shared meaning is the mutual understanding of a message between speaker and audience.
17. Context influences all aspects of public speaking.
18. A speech does not need a clearly defined goal to be effective.
19. Constructive feedback is not a useful tool for self-evaluation and improvement.

20. Very few people have a fear of public speaking.

21. Effective public speaking is an inborn talent.

22. Successful public speakers devote time and effort to preparation.

23. Public speaking is similar in many ways to engaging in an important conversation.

24. Effective speaking and effective writing both require a sense of who the audience is.

25. In general, spoken language is more formal than written language.

26. *Ethnocentrism* is the belief that the ways of one's own culture are superior to those of other cultures.

27. The practice of oratory, or rhetoric, emerged full force in Greece in the fifth century B.C.E.

28. According to Aristotle and Cicero, memory is one of the five parts of speech preparation.

29. *Delivery* refers to adapting speech information to the audience in order to make your case.

30. The five canons of rhetoric are invention, adaptation, arrangement, timing, and delivery.

MULTIPLE-CHOICE QUESTIONS

31. Benefits of public speaking do *not* include
    A) exploring and sharing values.
    B) honing thinking and listening skills.
    C) improving intrapersonal skills.
    D) accomplishing professional and personal goals.

32. A form of communication between two people is called
    A) mass communication.
    B) small group communication.
    C) dyadic communication.
    D) public speaking.

33. Factors that distinguish public speaking from other forms of communication include
    A) opportunities for feedback.
    B) level of preparation.
    C) degree of formality.
    D) all of the above.

34. Listeners do not want the speaker to care about their
    A) interests.
    B) appearance.
    C) desires.
    D) goals.

35. In this form of communication, the receiver is physically removed from the messenger, and feedback is delayed.
    A) mass communication
    B) small group communication
    C) public speaking
    D) dyadic communication

36. Which of the following is the least formal type of communication?
    A) mass communication
    B) small group communication
    C) dyadic communication
    D) public speaking

37. All communication events include
    A) a source and a message.
    B) only a message.
    C) a transmittal device.
    D) none of the above.

38. Which of the following represents the process a message goes through when it is received and interpreted?
    A) channel → receiver → decoding
    B) source → receiver → encoding → decoding
    C) source → encoding → receiver → decoding
    D) source → receiver → channel

39. Transforming ideas and thoughts into messages is called
    A) encoding.
    B) decoding.
    C) receiving.
    D) channeling.

40. The recipient of the source's message is
    A) the encoder.
    B) the channel.
    C) the receiver.
    D) all of the above.

41. The audience's response to a message is referred to as
    A) shared meaning.
    B) feedback.
    C) the medium.
    D) decoding.

42. Anything that influences the speaker, the audience, the speech, the occasion, or the situation is called
    A) context.
    B) goals.
    C) outcome.
    D) communication process.

43. When setting goals for a speech, the speaker should ask
   A) What do I want the audience to learn or believe?
   B) What do I personally want to achieve by delivering this speech?
   C) both A and B.
   D) neither A nor B.

44. The fear of public speaking
   A) is rare.
   B) is widespread.
   C) is an inherited trait.
   D) cannot be overcome.

45. Public speaking relies on the same basic principles as which type of communication?
   A) interviewing
   B) small group communication
   C) mass communication
   D) conversation

46. How does spoken language differ from written communication?
   A) Speakers use unfamiliar words and complex sentences.
   B) Oral language is less interactive than written language.
   C) Personal pronouns occur more frequently in spoken communication.
   D) All of the above are ways that spoken language differs from written communication.

47. The modes of persuasion used to appeal to an audience are called
   A) rhetorical proofs.
   B) logic.
   C) public speaking.
   D) writing skills.

48. Which of the following is true of spoken language?
   A) It is more conversational than written language.
   B) It always occurs in informal settings.
   C) Listeners expect spoken language to be more formal than written language.
   D) All of the above are true.

49. The belief that the ways of one's own culture are superior to those of other cultures is called
   A) ethnicity.
   B) ethnography.
   C) ethnocentrism.
   D) egocentrism.

50. Which of the following is *not* one of the five canons of rhetoric?
   A) invention
   B) delivery
   C) persuasion
   D) arrangement

51. *Invention* refers to
    A) adapting speech information to the audience in order to make your case.
    B) the way the speaker uses language to express the speech's ideas.
    C) practicing the speech until it can be artfully delivered.
    D) none of the above.

FILL-IN-THE-BLANK QUESTIONS

52. In a recent survey of employers, ______ communication skills ranked first among desired skills.

53. Deep-seated feelings and ideas about what is important in life are called ______.

54. A form of communication between two people, such as a conversation, is ______ communication.

55. ______ is the process of interpreting a message.

56. The mutual understanding of a message between the speaker and the audience is called ______.

57. ______ is the audience's verbal or nonverbal responses to a message.

58. ______, also called noise, is a barrier to communication that may be physical, emotional, psychological, or environmental.

59. The speech assignment, the physical setting, the quality of other speakers' presentations, and recent events are all part of ______.

60. ______ is the effect of a speech after it has been delivered and assessed.

61. The opposite of ethnocentrism is ______.

ESSAY AND SHORT ANSWER QUESTIONS

62. List and explain three benefits of public speaking.

63. Give an example of how public speaking will broaden your horizons and add to your knowledge of the world around you.

64. Explain how studying the craft of public speaking will hone your critical thinking and listening skills.

65. Describe how speaking in public will enable you to express your values and explore the values of others.

66. Explain how public speaking is similar to conversation.

67. Discuss the shared characteristics of mass communication and public speaking.

68. List and describe one similarity and one difference between public speaking and small group communication.

69. Explain why public speaking is usually more formal than other types of communication.

70. Give an example of interference in a public speaking situation.

71. Why is it important for speakers to clearly define their goals?

72. Define speech context.

73. List and describe the elements of the communication process.

74. List two ways in which public speaking and writing are similar.

75. Why is it important for a speaker to understand the viewpoints held by audience members?

76. How can a speaker make every audience member feel recognized and included?

77. List and describe three of the five canons of rhetoric.

ANSWER KEY FOR CHAPTER 1

1. True (p. 7)
2. True (p. 7)
3. True (p. 9)
4. True (p. 8)
5. False (p. 10)
6. True (p. 10)
7. False (p. 10)
8. True (p. 11)
9. True (p. 11)
10. True (p. 11)
11. False (p. 11)
12. True (p. 12)
13. True (p. 12)
14. False (p. 12)
15. False (p. 12)
16. True (p. 12)
17. True (p. 12)
18. False (p. 13)
19. False (p. 13)
20. False (p. 13)
21. False (p. 13)
22. True (p. 13)
23. True (p. 14)
24. True (p. 14)
25. False (p. 15)
26. True (p. 15)
27. True (p. 16)
28. True (p. 16)
29. False (p. 16)
30. False (p. 16)
31. C (pp. 7–8)
32. C (p. 8)
33. D (p. 9)
34. B (p. 9)
35. A (p. 8)
36. C (p. 10)
37. A (p. 10)
38. C (p. 11)
39. A (p. 11)
40. C (p. 11)
41. B (p. 11)
42. A (p. 12)
43. C (p. 13)
44. B (p. 13)
45. D (p. 14)
46. C (p. 15)
47. A (p. 14)
48. A (p. 15)
49. C (p. 15)
50. C (p. 16)
51. A (p. 16)
52. oral (p. 7)
53. values (p. 8)
54. dyadic (p. 8)
55. Decoding (p. 11)
56. shared meaning (p. 12)
57. Feedback (p. 11)
58. Interference (p. 12)
59. context (p. 12)
60. Outcome (p. 13)
61. cultural sensitivity (p. 15)
62. (No answer, pp. 7–8)
63. (No answer, pp. 7–8)
64. (No answer, p. 8)
65. (No answer, p. 8)
66. (No answer, pp. 9, 14)
67. (No answer, p. 9)
68. (No answer, p. 9)
69. (No answer, p. 10)
70. (No answer, p. 12)
71. (No answer, p. 13)
72. (No answer, p. 12)
73. (No answer, pp. 10–13)
74. (No answer, p. 14)
75. (No answer, p. 15)
76. (No answer, p. 15)
77. (No answer, p. 16)

2 *Giving It a Try: Preparing Your First Speech*

TRUE/FALSE QUESTIONS

1. The first step in creating a speech involves determining the purpose of the speech.
2. When selecting a speech topic, a speaker should be guided solely by the audience's interests.
3. Audience analysis is a highly systematic process of understanding the audience in relation to the speech topic and the speaking occasion.
4. The general purpose of a speech is usually only to inform the audience.
5. There are two general speech purposes: to inform and to persuade.
6. The specific purpose of a speech is the same as the general purpose.
7. The general purpose of a speech focuses more closely on the goal of the speech than the specific purpose does.
8. A thesis statement is a sentence that clearly expresses the central idea of a speech.
9. A speaker should always use the thesis statement as a guidepost to develop and support the speech's main points.
10. Forming a specific purpose for a speech occurs after you formulate your thesis statement.
11. An effective speech should be organized around four or five main points.
12. Supporting material for a speech lends credibility to the speaker's message.
13. Every speech has three major parts: an introduction, body, and conclusion.
14. An introduction serves to introduce the topic and the speaker and to tell the audience the specific purpose of the speech.
15. During the body of a speech, the speaker should alert the audience to the specific purpose of the speech.

16. The speech body contains the main points and subpoints of the speech.

17. Supporting material is used mostly during the body of the speech.

18. Supporting material can enhance a speaker's credibility.

19. In the conclusion, the speaker should restate the speech purpose and reiterate how the main points confirm it.

20. Ending the speech on a strong note is unlikely to affect the audience's response because audience members have already heard the main points of the speech and have made up their minds by the end.

21. An outline provides the framework on which to arrange main points in support of the thesis.

22. In a speech outline, coordinate points are given less weight than the main points they support.

23. A speaker should develop either a working outline or a speaking outline, but not both.

24. Presentation aids are always visual.

25. Presentation aids help the audience retain ideas and understand difficult concepts.

26. To deliver an effective speech, a speaker should practice the speech at least six times.

27. The success of a speech depends on the preparation and practice put forth by the speaker.

28. A tape recorder can be a helpful device to use when rehearsing a speech.

29. Speaking in a monotone means a speaker is using an unvarying, flat tone.

30. It is more important for ESL speakers to focus on eliminating their accents than on pronunciation and articulation.

MULTIPLE-CHOICE QUESTIONS

31. The first step in the speech process is
    - A) research.
    - B) stating the purpose.
    - C) developing points.
    - D) selecting a topic.

32. When selecting a speech topic, a speaker should first consider which of the following as a guide?
    - A) the time limit of the speech
    - B) his or her interests
    - C) serious issues
    - D) historical events

33. The first step in the speechmaking process is ______, and the last step is ______.
    A) analyzing the audience; considering presentation aids
    B) selecting a topic; practicing delivery of the speech
    C) stating the speech purpose; outlining the speech
    D) composing a thesis statement; gathering supporting materials

34. The demographic characteristics of an audience include
    A) the ratio of males to females.
    B) racial and ethnic representation.
    C) age variations.
    D) all of the above.

35. Audience analysis involves the study of an audience through techniques such as
    A) interviews and questionnaires.
    B) observation and tape-recording.
    C) surveys and assumptions.
    D) interviews and conjecture.

36. Audience analysis is a highly systematic process of getting to know the listeners relative to
    A) the topic and the speech occasion.
    B) the topic and the time limit.
    C) the speech occasion and the general purpose.
    D) the speech purpose and the time limit.

37. To inform, to persuade, and to mark a special occasion are the three types of
    A) general purposes.
    B) specific purposes.
    C) thesis statements.
    D) speech occasions.

38. Anne chose to give a speech to her classmates about categories of computer games. The general purpose of Anne's speech was
    A) to inform.
    B) to persuade.
    C) to mark a special occasion.
    D) none of the above.

The following four phrases pertain to a specific speech. Use the phrases to answer questions 39–41.

Phrase 1: the Department of Transportation (DOT)

Phrase 2: DOT programs available online to serve community members

Phrase 3: to inform

Phrase 4: to inform the audience about three online DOT programs for consumers—Hazardous Road Conditions, Vehicle Registration, and Driver's License Renewal—so that they will be able to use the services of these programs

39. Which phrase is the general purpose?
A) phrase 1
B) phrase 2
C) phrase 3
D) phrase 4

40. Which phrase is the narrowed topic?
A) phrase 1
B) phrase 2
C) phrase 3
D) phrase 4

41. Which phrase is the specific purpose?
A) phrase 1
B) phrase 2
C) phrase 3
D) phrase 4

42. The ______ is an explicit statement of what you expect your speech to accomplish.
A) general purpose
B) specific purpose
C) audience analysis
D) topic selection

43. An effective speech should be organized around ______ main points.
A) one or two
B) two or three
C) four or five
D) seven or eight

44. Supporting material illustrates main points by ______ the speaker's main ideas.
A) substituting
B) disproving
C) verifying
D) all of the above

45. When supporting material shows that the speaker's ideas are consistent with others' ideas and actual events, the material lends ______ to the speaker's message.
A) description
B) credibility
C) humor
D) orderliness

46. Which part of a speech sets the tone for the entire speech?
A) introduction
B) body
C) conclusion
D) outline

47. In which part of a speech should the speaker illustrate each main point using supporting material?
A) introduction
B) body
C) conclusion
D) outline

48. Which part of a speech represents the speaker's last opportunity to motivate listeners and memorably state the theme of the speech?
A) introduction
B) body
C) conclusion
D) outline

49. In an outline, what kinds of points support main points?
A) coordinate
B) subordinate
C) equivalent
D) superior

50. Outlines are based on the principle of
    A) coordination and subordination.
    B) general and specific purpose.
    C) primacy and recency.
    D) topic selection.

51. Which kind of outline is usually brief and contains key words or phrases?
    A) working
    B) speaking
    C) specific
    D) operational

52. Presentation aids
    A) summarize and highlight information.
    B) help the audience retain ideas and understand difficult concepts.
    C) provide dramatic emphasis.
    D) can do all of the above.

53. A speech should be practiced at least how many times?
    A) six
    B) seven
    C) eight
    D) nine

FILL-IN-THE-BLANK QUESTIONS

54. Selecting a topic is the ______ step in preparing a speech.

55. The process of ______ helps to determine how receptive the audience will be toward a given topic.

56. To inform, to persuade, to entertain, and to mark a special occasion are general speech ______.

57. After a speaker has identified the general and specific purposes of the speech, he or she should then write a concise ______ statement that identifies what the speech is about.

58. Newspaper editorials, Internet sites, and pictures are examples of places to locate ______ for a speech.

59. The introduction, body, and conclusion make up the three parts of a(n) ______.

60. The part of a speech that contains the main ideas and supporting material is the ______.

61. In an outline, ______ points are of equal importance and are indicated by their parallel alignment.

62. One of the most effective ways to evaluate your speech and bolster confidence during rehearsals is to use a(n) ______.

ESSAY AND SHORT ANSWER QUESTIONS

63. List two ways in which a speaker can select a topic.
64. How can a speaker analyze the audience?
65. Why is it important to identify the purpose of a speech?
66. What are the components of a good thesis statement?
67. Why should a speech be separated into its major parts?
68. Identify the functions of the introduction, body, and conclusion.
69. Explain the difference between a working outline and a speaking outline.
70. How do presentation aids benefit a speech?
71. Discuss the importance of practicing a speech.
72. Explain how using a tape recorder during speech rehearsals can bolster speaker confidence.

ANSWER KEY FOR CHAPTER 2

1. False (p. 18)
2. False (p. 18)
3. True (p. 19)
4. False (p. 19)
5. False (p. 19)
6. False (p. 20)
7. False (p. 20)
8. True (p. 20)
9. True (p. 20)
10. False (p. 20)
11. False (p. 20)
12. True (p. 21)
13. True (p. 21)
14. True (p. 21)
15. False (p. 21)
16. True (p. 21)
17. True (p. 21)
18. True (p. 21)
19. True (p. 22)
20. False (p. 22)
21. True (p. 22)
22. False (p. 22)
23. False (p. 23)
24. False (p. 24)
25. True (p. 24)
26. True (p. 24)
27. True (p. 24)
28. True (p. 25)
29. True (p. 25)
30. False (p. 26)
31. D (p. 18)
32. B (p. 18)
33. B (pp. 18, 24)
34. D (p. 19)
35. A (p. 19)
36. A (p. 19)
37. A (p. 19)
38. A (p. 19)
39. C (p. 19)
40. B (p. 19)
41. D (p. 20)
42. B (p. 20)
43. B (p. 20)
44. C (p. 21)
45. B (p. 21)
46. A (p. 21)
47. B (pp. 21–22)
48. C (p. 22)
49. B (p. 22)
50. A (p. 22)
51. B (p. 23)
52. D (p. 24)
53. A (p. 24)
54. first (p. 18)
55. audience analysis (p. 19)
56. purposes (p. 19)
57. thesis (p. 20)
58. supporting material (p. 21)
59. speech (p. 21)
60. body (p. 21)
61. coordinate (p. 22)
62. tape recorder (p. 25)
63. (No answer, p. 18)
64. (No answer, p. 19)
65. (No answer, pp. 19–20)
66. (No answer, p. 20)
67. (No answer, p. 21)
68. (No answer, pp. 21–22)
69. (No answer, p. 23)
70. (No answer, p. 24)
71. (No answer, p. 24)
72. (No answer, p. 25)

Listeners and Speakers 3

TRUE/FALSE QUESTIONS

1. The continual flow or feedback between speaker and listener is the circular response.
2. In any given communication situation, listeners will process information in exactly the same way.
3. Speaking is the communication activity that one does more than any other.
4. Selective perception is a process in which listeners pay attention to certain messages and ignore others.
5. Audience members usually listen carefully to a speaker even if they believe the message is of no consequence to them.
6. Active listening is focused and purposeful.
7. A listening distraction is anything that competes for attention that you are trying to give to something else.
8. Noise, movement, light, darkness, heat, and cold are all examples of internal distractions.
9. When you experience strong emotions as you listen, these can be considered distractions.
10. Scriptwriting usually occurs when we sense that our attitudes or opinions are being challenged.
11. In defensive listening, audience members decide to hear things that aren't actually said by the speaker.
12. Effective listening precedes effective rebuttal.
13. Laziness and overconfidence are concepts related to defensive listening.
14. Differences in dialects or accents, nonverbal cues, and physical appearance sometimes serve as cultural barriers to listening.
15. Active listeners listen for the speaker's main ideas and watch his or her nonverbal cues.

16. Setting listening goals helps listeners get the most from a listening situation.

17. Identifying a speaker's organizational pattern will help listeners understand the main points of a message.

18. Speakers should not identify their main points during the introduction of a speech.

19. Transitions can alert the listener that a main point is about to be discussed.

20. Much of the meaning of a message is communicated through nonverbal cues.

21. Facial expressions are not reliable cues that help people listen better.

22. Critical thinking is the ability to evaluate claims on the basis of well-supported reasons.

23. When evaluating evidence, the listener should determine if the sources of the evidence are credible.

24. Critical thinking does not involve assessing the logic of an argument.

25. When listening to a speech, it is important to consider different perspectives and realize that both the listener's and the speaker's perspectives are subject to error.

26. Listeners who do not like a speaker's topic are not required to be honest and fair in evaluating the speech.

27. Accents, awkward grammatical phrases, and unusual word choice are good reasons for listeners to "tune out" a speaker.

MULTIPLE-CHOICE QUESTIONS

28. Most people retain what percentage of what they hear immediately after listening?
    A) 25 percent
    B) 35 percent
    C) 50 percent
    D) 75 percent

29. A speech is successful when the speaker and listener together ______ the meaning of the speech.
    A) co-write
    B) co-create
    C) co-select
    D) co-associate

30. The conscious act of recognizing, understanding, and accurately interpreting messages communicated by others is called
    A) hearing.
    B) listening.
    C) circular response.
    D) the message-perception gap.

31. The reflexive or automatic process of perceiving sound is called
    A) hearing.
    B) listening.
    C) circular response.
    D) the message-perception gap.

32. Paying attention to information that is important to us, being interested in information that touches our own experiences and backgrounds, and sorting and filtering new information based on what we already know are key elements of
    A) imaginative listening.
    B) selective listening.
    C) simplistic listening.
    D) attentive listening.

33. Listeners tend to pay attention to
    A) information that they deem important.
    B) information that is associated with their experiences.
    C) information that relates to their backgrounds.
    D) all of the above.

34. Active listening is
    A) a vague, abstract multistep process.
    B) a focused, purposeful multistep process.
    C) a time-consuming one-step process.
    D) an active and engaging one-step system.

35. According to a recent study, the poor listening habits that rank highest among college students include
    A) oversimplified ideals, boredom, and voter apathy.
    B) imaginative listening and dogmatism.
    C) inattentiveness, defensive listening, and overconfidence.
    D) none of the above.

36. Distractions to listening can originate
    A) only outside of us.
    B) within our thoughts and feelings.
    C) both A and B.
    D) neither A nor B.

37. Construction noise, automobile traffic, slamming doors, and poor ventilation are examples of
    A) external distractions.
    B) internal distractions.
    C) defensive listening.
    D) inattentiveness.

38. Daydreaming, fatigue, illness, and strong emotions are examples of
    A) scriptwriting.
    B) internal distractions.
    C) external distractions.
    D) defensive listening.

39. Scriptwriters tend to
    A) focus on the speaker.
    B) concentrate on the speaker's motives.
    C) plan how they will respond to the speaker.
    D) employ external distractions.

40. Laziness and overconfidence in listening are manifested by
    A) expecting too little from the speaker.
    B) displaying an arrogant attitude.
    C) ignoring important information.
    D) all of the above.

41. In which of the following cultures is direct eye contact considered a sign of active listening and respect?
    A) United States
    B) Korea
    C) China
    D) none of the above

42. Active listeners
    A) are often distracting to other listeners.
    B) normally set listening goals and listen for main ideas.
    C) rely primarily on a speaker's verbal cues.
    D) apply the same goals to every speech.

43. When listening for main ideas, a listener should
    A) ignore the speaker's organizational pattern.
    B) take into account only the introduction, transitions, and conclusion.
    C) take notes of the speaker's main points.
    D) do none of the above.

44. If a speaker's verbal and nonverbal messages do not correspond, which cues are usually perceived by the listener as being the most honest?
    A) verbal
    B) nonverbal
    C) selective
    D) listening echoes

45. ______ involves evaluating evidence, analyzing assumptions and biases, assessing the logic of an argument, and resisting false assumptions.
    A) Critical thinking
    B) Bridging the message-perception gap
    C) Minimizing distractions
    D) Eliminating cultural barriers

FILL-IN-THE-BLANK QUESTIONS

46. ______ is the continual flow or feedback between speaker and listener.

47. Paying attention to certain messages and ignoring other messages is called ______.

48. Anything that competes for the attention that you are trying to give to something else is called a listening ______.

49. Setting listening ______ helps active listeners get the most from the speaker's message.

50. Statements that alert the audience that the speaker is moving to the next main point are called ______.

51. The ability to evaluate a speaker's ideas based on well-supported reasons is a component of ______.

52. Unsupported conclusions are also known as ______.

53. If you find a speaker dull or too serious but still pay attention to the speech, you have adjusted to the speaker's ______.

ESSAY AND SHORT ANSWER QUESTIONS

54. Describe the factors that influence listening.

55. Explain why people sort and filter information based on what they already know.

56. Describe how a listener can plan ways of coping with common listening distractions.

57. Describe two types of internal distractions, and explain how they detract from a communication situation.

58. Define *defensive listening* and prescribe two ways to eliminate it.

59. How does scriptwriting differ from defensive listening?

60. Identify something you perceive to be a cultural barrier to listening, based on your own experience or a hypothetical situation.

61. Write a brief list of ways you can become a more active listener. Tailor these goals to reflect your own strengths and weaknesses as a listener.

62. Explain why listeners may sometimes give more credence to nonverbal cues than to verbal messages.

63. Define *critical thinking* and explain why it is important in the process of communicating with others.

64. Identify three guidelines for evaluating speeches and presentations.

65. When you evaluate a speech, how can you be compassionate and constructive in your criticism?

ANSWER KEY FOR CHAPTER 3

1. True (p. 38)
2. False (p. 38)
3. False (p. 38)
4. True (p. 38)
5. False (p. 39)
6. True (p. 40)
7. True (p. 40)
8. False (p. 40)
9. True (p. 41)
10. False (p. 41)
11. False (pp. 41–42)
12. True (p. 42)
13. True (p. 42)
14. True (p. 42)
15. True (p. 43)
16. True (p. 43)
17. True (p. 44)
18. False (p. 44)
19. True (p. 44)
20. True (p. 45)
21. False (p. 45)
22. True (p. 45)
23. True (p. 45)
24. False (p. 46)
25. True (p. 46)
26. False (p. 47)
27. False (p. 47)
28. C (p. 38)
29. B (p. 38)
30. B (p. 38)
31. A (p. 38)
32. B (pp. 38–39)
33. D (p. 39)
34. B (p. 40)
35. C (p. 40)
36. C (pp. 40–41)
37. A (p. 40)
38. B (p. 41)
39. C (p. 41)
40. D (p. 42)
41. A (p. 42)
42. B (p. 43)
43. C (p. 44)
44. B (p. 45)
45. A (pp. 45–46)
46. Circular response (p. 38)
47. selective perception (p. 38)
48. distraction (p. 40)
49. goals (p. 43)
50. transitions (p. 44)
51. critical thinking (p. 45)
52. overgeneralizations (p. 46)
53. style (p. 47)
54. (No answer, p. 39)
55. (No answer, p. 39)
56. (No answer, p. 40)
57. (No answer, p. 41)
58. (No answer, pp. 41–42)
59. (No answer, pp. 41–42)
60. (No answer, p. 42)
61. (No answer, pp. 43–45)
62. (No answer, p. 45)
63. (No answer, pp. 45–46)
64. (No answer, p. 47)
65. (No answer, p. 47)

Ethical Public Speaking 4

TRUE/FALSE QUESTIONS

1. Defamation is the study of moral conduct or of how people should act toward one another.
2. Public speakers are in a position to influence others but are not responsible for the effect their words have on listeners.
3. The Greek word *ethos* means character.
4. The First Amendment of the U.S. Constitution guarantees freedom of speech.
5. Listeners tend to distrust speakers who do not appear credible.
6. If a particular type of speech is legal, it is also ethical.
7. For the most part, values are culturally determined and are transmitted through social institutions and organizations.
8. Most values are learned late in life and tend to remain with individuals for a short period of time.
9. Successful speeches appeal to the listeners' values.
10. As a speaker, you should assume that listeners hold the same values as your own.
11. According to Milton Rokeach, terminal values are valued characteristics that people can possess.
12. The qualities of dignity and integrity are central to ethical speech.
13. Trustworthiness is a combination of honesty and dependability.
14. To show respect for their listeners, speakers should promote in-group and out-group distinctions.
15. A respectful speaker focuses on personalities as well as on issues.
16. Ethnocentrism is the belief that the cultural ways of others are better than one's own cultural ways.

17. Manipulating information to achieve a particular purpose is not always unethical.

18. Acknowledging sources is an essential aspect of ethical speechmaking.

19. Racist, sexist, and ageist slurs are forms of hate speech.

20. Hate speech promotes in-group and out-group distinctions.

21. A stereotype is a generalization about an apparent characteristic of a group that is applied to all members of that group.

22. Hate speech relies on stereotypes but not on prejudice.

23. When supported by facts, emotional appeals are a legitimate way for a speaker to achieve his or her goal.

24. The quality of fairness in a speaker refers to his or her effort to see all sides of an issue and be open-minded.

25. Any source that requires credit in written form should be acknowledged in oral form.

26. The severe consequences of plagiarism apply to the academic but not the professional world.

27. Plagiarism is the act of crediting sources in a speech.

28. Verbatim statements are known as paraphrases.

29. It is not necessary to acknowledge direct quotations in a speech.

30. Paraphrasing alters the form but not the substance of another person's ideas.

MULTIPLE-CHOICE QUESTIONS

31. Which of the following is a Greek word meaning "character"?
    A) logos
    B) ethos
    C) pathos
    D) mythos

32. The study of moral conduct, or how people should act toward one another, is termed
    A) ethics.
    B) ethnology.
    C) ethnography.
    D) ethnicity.

33. The following comprise a positive ethos:
    A) competence, charisma, and candor.
    B) competence, dramatic ability, and charisma.
    C) competence, good moral character, and goodwill.
    D) competence, candor, and good moral character.

34. Research on speaker credibility reveals that people most trust those speakers who
    A) have a sound grasp of the subject.
    B) display sound reasoning.
    C) are honest and not manipulative.
    D) have all of the preceding qualities.

35. The ______ Amendment assures protection to both honest and dishonest speakers.
    A) First
    B) Third
    C) Second
    D) Fourth

36. Which of the following types of speech are legally protected in the United States?
    A) racist and sexist speech
    B) pornographic speech
    C) both A and B
    D) neither A nor B

37. An ethical speaker is conscious of ______ values.
    A) the speaker's
    B) the speaker's and the university's
    C) the speaker's and the audience's
    D) the speaker's and all other people's

38. An example of a terminal value or characteristic is
    A) ambitious.
    B) courageous.
    C) logical.
    D) happiness.

39. ______ values are desirable ends in themselves, whereas ______ values are valued characteristics that people can possess.
    A) Instrumental; ethical
    B) Terminal; instrumental
    C) Ethical; terminal
    D) Cultural; ethical

40. A person's feeling of self-worth or self-respect is called
    A) trustworthiness.
    B) dignity.
    C) integrity.
    D) candor.

41. An incorruptible speaker, or one who will not compromise solely to persuade others, possesses
    A) trustworthiness.
    B) dignity.
    C) integrity.
    D) candor.

42. A speaker who is both honest and dependable has the quality of
    A) trustworthiness.
    B) dignity.
    C) integrity.
    D) candor.

43. A speaker who is trustworthy
    A) does not use misleading information.
    B) reveals his or her true purpose.
    C) both A and B.
    D) neither A nor B.

44. Which of the following is *not* a way for a speaker to display respect for the audience?
    A) Focus on issues rather than personalities.
    B) Address issues only from one's own point of view.
    C) Avoid in-group and out-group distinctions.
    D) Allow the audience the power of rational choice.

45. Speakers who use jargon in their speeches
    A) create both in-group and out-group distinctions.
    B) compel the audience to be more interested in the topic.
    C) risk excluding some audience members' understanding of the message.
    D) do all of the above.

46. Hate speech is offensive communication that is most directed against
    A) political ideas.
    B) people's values.
    C) people's racial, ethnic, religious, gender, or other characteristics.
    D) people's psychological characteristics.

47. If a source used in a speech requires credit in written form, it also
    A) requires consent from the author.
    B) should be mentioned before the speaker's findings.
    C) needs to be quoted directly.
    D) should be acknowledged orally as another person's work.

48. To conduct a plagiarism check for your speech, you should do all of the following *except*
    A) acknowledge other people's research and evidence.
    B) acknowledge your own ideas and opinions.
    C) acknowledge direct quotations.
    D) acknowledge paraphrased information.

FILL-IN-THE-BLANK QUESTIONS

49. The Greek word for *character* from which the word *ethics* is derived is ______.

50. The right to be free from unreasonable constraints on expression is called ______.

51. ______ are people's most enduring judgments about what is good or bad, important or unimportant.

52. A person's feeling of worth, honor, or respect is called ______.

53. ______ is a quality that combines honesty and dependability.

54. A word that means "treating people right" is ______.

55. The word ______ refers to specialized terminology.

56. ______ is offensive communication directed against people's race, ethnic origin, religion, gender, or other characteristics.

57. Cutting and pasting material directly from other sources and representing it as your own is ______ plagiarism.

58. Copying material into your speech draft from a source and then changing and rearranging the material to make it appear as your own is ______ plagiarism.

59. If a person uses someone else's ideas or words without acknowledging the source, he or she is committing ______.

60. To ______ is to restate someone else's ideas, opinions, or theories in the speaker's own words.

ESSAY AND SHORT ANSWER QUESTIONS

61. Why are ethics important to the speechmaking process?

62. Identify three personal values that you feel you have in common with your classmates.

63. List two terminal values that are significant to you, and explain why.

64. List two instrumental values that are significant to you, and explain why.

65. How can a speaker display the qualities of dignity and integrity during a speech?

66. How can a speaker demonstrate his or her trustworthiness to the audience?

67. Give an example of a stereotype.

68. Define *plagiarism* and provide an example.

69. List two elements of information that a speaker should provide when citing sources during a speech.

70. Paraphrase this quotation: "The tongue weighs practically nothing, therefore people can hold it."

71. How should a speaker appropriately credit online sources?

ANSWER KEY FOR CHAPTER 4

1. False (p. 49)
2. False (p. 49)
3. True (p. 49)
4. True (p. 50)
5. True (p. 50)
6. False (pp. 50–51)
7. True (p. 51)
8. False (p. 51)
9. True (p. 52)
10. False (p. 52)
11. False (p. 53)
12. True (p. 54)
13. True (p. 54)
14. False (p. 55)
15. False (p. 55)
16. False (p. 55)
17. False (p. 54)
18. True (p. 54)
19. True (p. 55)
20. True (p. 55)
21. True (p. 55)
22. False (p. 55)
23. True (p. 57)
24. True (p. 58)
25. True (p. 58)
26. False (p. 58)
27. False (p. 58)
28. False (p. 59)
29. False (p. 59)
30. True (pp. 59–60)
31. B (p. 49)
32. A (p. 49)
33. C (p. 49)
34. D (p. 50)
35. A (p. 50)
36. C (p. 51)
37. C (pp. 51–52)
38. D (p. 53)
39. B (p. 53)
40. B (p. 54)
41. C (p. 54)
42. A (p. 54)
43. C (p. 54)
44. B (p. 55)
45. C (p. 55)
46. C (p. 55)
47. D (p. 58)
48. B (pp. 58–60)
49. ethos (p. 49)
50. free speech (p. 50)
51. Values (p. 51)
52. dignity (p. 54)
53. Trustworthiness (p. 54)
54. respect (p. 55)
55. jargon (p. 55)
56. Hate speech (p. 55)
57. wholesale (p. 58)
58. patchwrite (p. 58)
59. plagiarism (p. 58)
60. paraphrase (p. 59)
61. (No answer, p. 49)
62. (No answer, pp. 52–53)
63. (No answer, p. 53)
64. (No answer, p. 53)
65. (No answer, p. 54)
66. (No answer, p. 54)
67. (No answer, p. 55)
68. (No answer, p. 58)
69. (No answer, pp. 59–60)
70. (No answer, pp. 59–60)
71. (No answer, p. 59)

Managing Speech Anxiety 5

TRUE/FALSE QUESTIONS

1. When properly channeled, a speaker's nervousness can boost his or her performance.
2. Public speaking anxiety, or PSA, can refer to a speaker's fear or anxiety associated with anticipated communication to an audience.
3. Lack of experience does not generally increase a speaker's public speaking anxiety.
4. The audience is likely to see the speaker more critically than the speaker sees himself or herself.
5. When speakers focus on themselves, they become less sensitive to things that might be wrong with their performance.
6. The onset of public speaking anxiety can occur as early as when a speaker first learns that he or she will have to give a speech.
7. Pre-preparation anxiety usually occurs when a speaker rehearses the speech.
8. Performance anxiety in speechmaking is usually most pronounced as the speech builds to its climax.
9. For ESL speakers, practicing oral English does not help in mastering the language.
10. Preparation and practice can help you deliver a good speech, but cannot help to alleviate public speaking anxiety
11. Having a positive attitude toward speechmaking results in a raised heart rate during delivery of a speech.
12. Thinking of public speaking as a threat can be part of positive thinking about public speaking, since such thoughts give speakers an edge and improve their public speaking performance.
13. Thinking about your speech as an extension of ordinary conversation rather than as a performance will help you achieve a more positive, relaxed outlook on public speaking.
14. Visualization is not an effective technique for building speaker confidence.

15. When you feel stressed, the center of your breathing tends to move from the upper chest to the back of the throat, leaving you with a reduced supply of air.

16. In stress-control breathing, the center of breathing is felt in the back of the throat.

17. Stage One of stress-control breathing involves using a calming word in a mantra.

18. Practicing natural gestures is a relaxation technique.

19. The most effective speakers stand perfectly still behind a podium and do not walk around.

20. A speaker's movement serves to relieve tension and helps to hold the audience's attention.

21. Your speech performance evaluation is a reflection of the kind of person you are.

22. Giving a speech can be a satisfying and empowering experience.

MULTIPLE-CHOICE QUESTIONS

23. In some surveys conducted to determine the greatest fears among humans, what did public speaking outrank?
    A) death
    B) snakes
    C) spiders
    D) all of the above

24. Feeling ______ is one reason many people are uncomfortable about public speaking.
    A) attractive
    B) superior to the audience
    C) different
    D) depersonalized

25. A speaker's general fear or anxiety associated with either actual or anticipated communication to an audience is known as
    A) communication nervousness.
    B) communication uneasiness.
    C) public speaking anxiety.
    D) stage fright.

26. ______ is the acronym for the fear associated with a speaker's communication to an audience.
    A) PSA
    B) APA
    C) MLA
    D) ABD

27. Feeling conspicuous when delivering a speech
    A) does not bother most public speakers.
    B) is common among politicians.
    C) makes a speaker feel anxious about being the center of attention.
    D) none of the above.

28. Tyson began to panic as soon as his instructor gave the speech assignment to the class. Tyson experienced
    A) pre-preparation anxiety.
    B) preparation anxiety.
    C) pre-performance anxiety.
    D) performance anxiety.

29. Claire began to feel nervous once she began organizing and writing her speech. Which type of anxiety did Claire experience?
    A) pre-preparation anxiety
    B) preparation anxiety
    C) pre-performance anxiety
    D) performance anxiety

30. Each of the following is a successful strategy for gaining public speaking confidence *except*
    A) modifying thoughts and attitudes.
    B) personalizing the speech evaluation.
    C) seeking pleasure in the occasion.
    D) practicing the speech.

31. If English is not a speaker's first language, which of the following should the speaker do?
    A) speak as quickly as possible
    B) practice difficult words in English
    C) learn and utilize jargon
    D) all of the above

32. Which of the following does *not* appear on the Preparation and Practice Checklist?
    A) Plan time for library research.
    B) Prepare for the speech evaluation.
    C) Rehearse your speech.
    D) Check out the site where you will be speaking.

33. Which of the following is *not* true of visualizing?
    A) It strengthens your positive attitude.
    B) It is a highly effective technique for building public speaking confidence.
    C) It involves the mental exercise of seeing yourself give a successful speech.
    D) It involves physically going through the motions of giving your speech.

34. ______ techniques are to public speaking anxiety what warm-ups are to exercise.
    A) Relaxation
    B) Concentration
    C) Manipulation
    D) Focus

35. Helpful relaxation techniques for public speakers include
    A) movement.
    B) stress-motivated breathing.
    C) artificial gestures.
    D) all of the above.

36. Jasper received some personal criticism from audience members after delivering his speech. Instead of taking their remarks personally, Jasper chose to concentrate on comments that focused on his speech, not himself. Jasper correctly opted to ______ the speech evaluation.
    A) depersonalize
    B) personify
    C) decode
    D) visualize

FILL-IN-THE-BLANK QUESTIONS

37. Feeling different from the audience, a lack of public speaking experience, and uneasiness about being the center of attention can lead to ______.

38. Katarina experienced ______ anxiety as soon as she first learned that she had to give a speech.

39. The onset of nervousness that occurs during the rehearsal of a speech is called ______ anxiety.

40. The type of anxiety that is most pronounced during the introduction phase of a speech is termed ______ anxiety.

41. As Bizhi prepared to give her speech, she mentally pictured herself giving a successful speech. To build confidence, Bizhi was practicing ______.

42. A form of breathing in which the center of breathing is felt in the stomach rather than in the chest is called ______ breathing.

ESSAY AND SHORT ANSWER QUESTIONS

43. Explain why public speaking is such a source of anxiety for most people.

44. Explain how being the center of attention can contribute to an uncomfortable speech situation.

45. Describe some ways a speaker feels conspicuous when presenting a speech.

46. Identify the type of public speaking anxiety that affects you most, and describe how you cope with it.

47. List two times that PSA can occur in the speechmaking process.

48. How can speakers increase their confidence by changing their thinking about public speaking from a "performance orientation" to a "communication orientation"?

49. Write a brief account of how you can use visualization to build public speaking confidence.

50. Discuss two relaxation techniques that public speakers can use to help reduce public speaking anxiety.

51. Identify the relaxation technique that is most helpful to you as a public speaker. Explain how it has helped you.

ANSWER KEY FOR CHAPTER 5

1. True (p. 63)
2. True (p. 63)
3. False (pp. 63–64)
4. False (p. 65)
5. False (p. 65)
6. True (p. 65)
7. False (p. 66)
8. False (p. 66)
9. False (p. 67)
10. False (p. 67)
11. False (p. 68)
12. False (p. 69)
13. True (p. 69)
14. False (p. 69)
15. False (p. 70)
16. False (p. 70)
17. False (p. 70)
18. True (p. 70)
19. False (p. 70)
20. True (p. 70)
21. False (p. 71)
22. True (p. 71)
23. D (p. 63)
24. C (p. 63)
25. C (p. 65)
26. A (p. 65)
27. C (p. 65)
28. A (p. 65)
29. B (p. 66)
30. B (pp. 66–71)
31. B (p. 67)
32. B (p. 68)
33. D (p. 69)
34. A (p. 70)
35. A (p. 70)
36. A (p. 71)
37. public speaking anxiety (p. 63)
38. pre-preparation (p. 65)
39. pre-performance (p. 66)
40. performance (p. 66)
41. visualization (p. 69)
42. stress-control (p. 70)
43. (No answer, pp. 63–64)
44. (No answer, pp. 64–65)
45. (No answer, p. 65)
46. (No answer, pp. 65–71)
47. (No answer, pp. 65–66)
48. (No answer, p. 69)
49. (No answer, p. 69)
50. (No answer, p. 70)
51. (No answer, p. 70)

Analyzing the Audience 6

TRUE/FALSE QUESTIONS

1. Audience analysis is the process of gathering and analyzing information about listeners.
2. It is important for a speaker to understand an audience's beliefs and attitudes, but not their values.
3. Being *audience-centered* means abandoning your own convictions and catering mainly to audience concerns.
4. Beliefs reflect a predisposition to respond to people, ideas, objects, or events in evaluative ways.
5. Values are based on attitudes.
6. Beliefs are shaped by values.
7. People's most enduring judgments about what is good and bad in life are called *attitudes.*
8. A speaker should try to uncover the audience's feelings toward the speech topic, the speaker, and the speech occasion.
9. As a general rule, people give more interest and attention to topics about which they have a negative attitude.
10. An audience that holds negative attitudes toward the speaker will tend to disregard even the most important or interesting message.
11. To create positive audience attitudes toward the speaker, the speaker should display the characteristics of a credible speaker.
12. A voluntary audience presents more challenges than a captive audience, because they are likely to have higher expectations.
13. All audience members bring the same set of expectations and emotions to a speech event.
14. A speaker who fails to consider the audience's expectations risks alienating audience members.

15. If audience members are negatively disposed toward your topic, as a speaker you should provide them with good reasons for why their attitudes are unfounded.

16. Demographics are the psychological characteristics of a given population.

17. Speech topics should be relevant to the age interests of an audience.

18. Gender is not a demographic characteristic.

19. The term *co-culture* refers to a social community whose perspectives and style of communicating may or may not differ from one's own.

20. Thinking of females as nurturers and caregivers is an example of a gender stereotype.

21. Understanding the listeners' ethnic and cultural composition is important in delivering a successful speech.

22. The cultural patterns of behavior identified by Hofstede are called *value dimensions.*

23. Collectivist cultures view personal identity, needs, and desires as secondary to those of the larger group.

24. Cultures with high levels of power distance place greater value on social equality.

25. *Uncertainty avoidance* refers to the extent to which people feel threatened by ambiguity.

26. Traditional feminine traits include ambition and earning power.

27. Culture influences our values.

28. The dominant values in the United States rank higher in masculinity than in femininity.

29. The United States and Australia are individualistic cultures.

30. Socioeconomic status includes income, occupation, and education.

31. Income is a demographic factor that does not pervasively affect people's life experiences.

32. Occupational interests are tied to politics, the economy, education, and social reform.

33. Generally, people with higher levels of education tend to be more willing to change their beliefs.

34. Being aware of an audience's general religious orientation can help a speaker know how the audience will respond to controversial topics.

35. Political issues are usually not touchy subjects for most audiences.

36. Interviews and surveys are the only methods of audience analysis.

37. For audience analysis, interviews generally take less time to implement than do surveys.

38. In a survey questionnaire, fixed alternative questions measure the respondent's level of agreement or disagreement with specific issues.

39. The Gallup Poll and the National Opinion Research Center are two of the most active and reputable polling organizations.

40. Published sources are helpful in conducting audience analysis.

41. The physical setting in which a speech occurs can have a significant impact on the outcome of a speech.

42. It is not usually helpful to a speaker to know the audience's seating arrangement.

MULTIPLE-CHOICE QUESTIONS

43. The study of audience members' attitudes, beliefs, values, and personality traits is known as audience
    A) sociology.
    B) demographics.
    C) apprehension.
    D) psychology.

44. Betraying your beliefs and convictions in order to appeal to the audience is known as
    A) being audience centered.
    B) pandering.
    C) captivating the audience.
    D) analyzing the audience.

45. Which of the following would be considered an attitude rather than a belief or a value?
    A) "I believe in God."
    B) "I like rap music."
    C) "Honesty is essential to friendship."
    D) "Life should be financially secure."

46. Values are
    A) our conceptions of what is true and false.
    B) our predispositions to respond to things in evaluative ways.
    C) our perceptions of reality.
    D) our most enduring judgments about what is good and bad in life.

47. A speaker should try to uncover the audience's feelings toward
    A) the speech topic.
    B) the speaker.
    C) the speech occasion.
    D) all of the above.

48. Which of the following techniques can help create a sense of audience identification with the speaker?
    A) sharing a relevant, personal story
    B) emphasizing a shared role
    C) dressing like the audience
    D) all of the above

49. Which of the following would *not* be considered a demographic characteristic?
    A) gender
    B) ethnic or cultural background
    C) self-esteem
    D) religion

50. The statistical characteristics of a given population or group of people are known as
    A) psychographics.
    B) demographics.
    C) profiles.
    D) beliefs.

51. How many demographic characteristics are typically considered in the analysis of speech audiences?
    A) three
    B) four
    C) five
    D) six

52. Which of the following countries does *not* rank high on individualism?
    A) Venezuela
    B) Australia
    C) Great Britain
    D) Canada

53. Which cultures structure life more rigidly and formally for their members?
    A) low-uncertainty avoidance cultures
    B) high-uncertainty avoidance cultures
    C) low power distance cultures
    D) high masculine cultures

54. India, Brazil, Greece, and Mexico are countries that are high in their level of
    A) low-uncertainty avoidance.
    B) high power distance.
    C) collectivism.
    D) none of the above.

55. Socioeconomic status (SES) includes
    A) gender, occupation, and religion.
    B) ethnicity, education, and occupation.
    C) income, occupation, and education.
    D) none of the above.

56. Tools that a speaker can use to analyze an audience include
    A) interviews.
    B) surveys.
    C) published sources.
    D) all of the above.

57. If you ask survey respondents to respond to questions with a limited choice of answers, you are asking what type of questions?
A) interview
B) fixed alternative
C) scale
D) open-ended

58. ______ allow a mix of open-ended and closed-ended questions.
A) Interviews
B) Surveys
C) Both A and B
D) Written sources

59. In an interview, what types of questions are particularly useful for probing beliefs and opinions?
A) closed-ended
B) fixed alternative
C) scale
D) open-ended

60. Interview questions that invite elaboration are ______ questions.
A) open-ended
B) closed-ended
C) confidential
D) scale

61. Which types of questions on a survey may be either fixed alternative or scale questions?
A) open-ended
B) closed-ended
C) analytical
D) potential

62. Characteristics of the speech setting include
A) the size of the audience and the length of the speech.
B) lighting and sound.
C) seating capacity and arrangement.
D) all of the above.

FILL-IN-THE-BLANK QUESTIONS

63. Audience analysis is the process by which a speaker discovers the needs and interests of a particular audience regarding the speech ______.

64. Audience members' attitudes, beliefs, values, and personality traits make up audience ______.

65. The ______ audience are the individuals within the broader audience whom you are most likely to influence in the direction you seek.

66. ______ stereotypes are oversimplified and often distorted ideas about the innate nature of men or women.

67. Interviews and surveys are appropriate tools for audience ______.

68. A(n) ______ is a form of face-to-face communication for the purpose of gathering information.

69. Questions that seek no particular response and allow respondents to elaborate as much as they wish are known as ______ questions.

70. Questions that measure the respondent's level of agreement or disagreement with particular issues are called ______ questions.

71. Location, time, seating arrangements, light, and sound are all components of the physical speech ______.

ESSAY AND SHORT ANSWER QUESTIONS

72. Explain the relationship among attitudes, beliefs, and values.

73. Why are audience demographics an important source of information for a speaker?

74. Using your own experience, discuss an example of a gender stereotype.

75. Identify two value dimensions and explain them.

76. Define socioeconomic status (SES), and explain its importance in the process of audience analysis.

77. Use an example to explain how religion can be a powerful predictor of audience response.

78. Identify the thesis statement for your last (or next) speech. Then imagine that you are conducting a survey on this speech topic. List four fixed-alternative survey questions that would be appropriate for your speech, audience, and topic.

79. Identify the thesis statement for your last (or next) speech. Then imagine that you are conducting a survey on this speech topic. List four scale survey questions that would be appropriate for your speech. audience, and topic.

80. Provide two examples of an open-ended interview question.

81. Why should a speaker spend time becoming familiar with the speech setting before giving a speech?

82. Discuss how the seating arrangement can affect a speaker's audience.

83. What is the speech context, and how does it affect the audience's reception of a speech?

ANSWER KEY FOR CHAPTER 6

1. True (p. 78)
2. False (p. 79)
3. False (p. 78)
4. False (p. 79)
5. False (p. 79)
6. True (p. 79)
7. False (p. 79)
8. True (p. 80)
9. False (p. 80)
10. True (pp. 80–81)
11. True (p. 81)
12. False (p. 81)
13. False (p. 81)
14. True (p. 81)
15. True (p. 80)
16. False (p. 82)
17. True (p. 82)
18. False (p. 82)
19. True (p. 83)
20. True (p. 88)
21. True (p. 83)
22. True (p. 83)
23. True (p. 83)
24. False (p. 84)
25. True (p. 83)
26. False (p. 84)
27. True (p. 84)
28. True (p. 84)
29. True (p. 83)
30. True (p. 85)
31. False (p. 85)
32. True (p. 86)
33. True (p. 86)
34. True (p. 86)
35. False (p. 86)
36. False (p. 88)
37. False (p. 88)
38. False (p. 89)
39. True (p. 91)
40. True (p. 91)
41. True (p. 92)
42. False (p. 92)
43. D (pp. 78–79)
44. B (p. 78)
45. B (p. 79)
46. D (p. 79)
47. D (p. 80)
48. D (p. 81)
49. C (p. 82)
50. B (p. 82)
51. D (p. 82)
52. A (p. 83)
53. B (p. 83)
54. B (p. 84)
55. C (p. 85)
56. D (pp. 88–91)
57. B (p. 89)
58. C (pp. 88–89)
59. D (p. 89)
60. A (p. 89)
61. B (p. 89)
62. D (pp. 91–92)
63. topic (p. 78)
64. psychology (p. 78)
65. target (p. 82)
66. Gender (p. 88)
67. analysis (p. 88)
68. interview (p. 88)
69. open-ended (p. 89)
70. scale (p. 89)
71. setting (pp. 91–92)
72. (No answer, p. 79)
73. (No answer, pp. 81–88)
74. (No answer, p. 88)
75. (No answer, p. 83)
76. (No answer, pp. 85–88)
77. (No answer, p. 86)
78. (No answer, p. 89)
79. (No answer, p. 89)
80. (No answer, p. 89)
81. (No answer, pp. 91–92)
82. (No answer, p. 92)
83. (No answer, p. 92)

7 *Selecting a Topic and Purpose*

TRUE/FALSE QUESTIONS

1. As long as your speech topic interests you, it will be appropriate to the audience and occasion.

2. In most instances, a speaker will be required to meet time constraints for a speech.

3. When a speaker chooses a speech topic, he or she is not held accountable for accomplishing a particular purpose.

4. The three general speech purposes are to inform, to persuade, and to entertain.

5. The general purpose of a speech is sometimes defined by the occasion.

6. A speech that describes, defines, explains, or demonstrates is persuasive in nature.

7. When selecting a topic for an informative speech, the speaker should try to gauge what the audience already knows about the topic.

8. Speaking over or under audience members' heads does not affect their attention to a speech.

9. If the audience is familiar with a speech topic, the speaker should attempt to present the knowledge in a fresh and interesting way.

10. The general purpose of a persuasive speech is to effect some degree of change in the audience.

11. Controversial issues are generally most appropriate for informative speeches.

12. A eulogy is a type of special occasion speech.

13. To develop an interesting speech, a speaker should choose a topic with which he or she is unfamiliar.

14. Current events are generally considered boring choices for speech topics.

15. Grassroots issues are interesting topic choices for speakers.

16. A common topic, such as gun control, is a good choice for a speech, because it touches upon a subject the audience is likely familiar with.

17. Brainstorming is a problem-solving technique involving the spontaneous generation of ideas.

18. Brainstorming is not an effective way to narrow a speech topic.

19. A topic map is a helpful way to visualize ideas for a speech.

20. To narrow a speech topic, you need to consider time constraints, audience expectations, and the nature of the occasion.

21. The specific speech purpose focuses more closely on the speech's goal than does the general speech purpose.

22. Speech topic choices should always be guided by ethical considerations.

23. The thesis statement is the theme or central idea of the speech.

24. If a speech is informative, its thesis statement does not propose that claims made are true or believed.

25. A well-written thesis statement aids the speaker in developing a coherent, understandable speech.

26. A thesis statement should be developed after you have developed all of your main points and supporting material.

MULTIPLE-CHOICE QUESTIONS

27. Speech topics may be
    A) assigned.
    B) self-selected.
    C) either A or B.
    D) neither A nor B.

28. If a speaker is asked to "make the audience laugh," the speaker has been given a
    A) time constraint.
    B) purpose.
    C) topic.
    D) challenge.

29. The ______ speech purpose answers the question, "Why am I speaking on this topic for this particular audience and occasion?"
    A) general
    B) specific
    C) informative
    D) persuasive

30. The purpose of a(n) ______ speech is to increase the audience's understanding and awareness of a topic.
    A) commemorative
    B) persuasive
    C) informative
    D) challenge

31. A persuasive speech topic is most appropriate when
   A) the audience holds attitudes and beliefs about the topic similar to the speaker's but needs direction in taking action.
   B) the audience feels the same about the topic as the speaker.
   C) the audience disagrees with the speaker's position and is likely to encounter opposing information in the near future.
   D) all of the above.

32. Special occasion speeches include all of the following except
   A) speeches of introduction.
   B) class lectures.
   C) speeches of presentation.
   D) acceptance speeches.

33. Personal interests for a speech topic include
   A) favorite activities and hobbies.
   B) goals and values.
   C) both A and B.
   D) neither A nor B.

34. Grassroots issues are
   A) poor speech topic choices.
   B) issues that don't affect the audience directly.
   C) usually local in nature.
   D) both B and C.

35. You stand a better chance of positively engaging your teacher and classmates if you choose a topic that is
   A) novel.
   B) controversial.
   C) common.
   D) based on general knowledge.

36. Which of the following is *not* a common or effective brainstorming technique?
   A) making lists
   B) refining topic purpose
   C) topic mapping
   D) using word association

37. Topic mapping is useful for ______ ideas for speech topics.
   A) visualizing
   B) defining
   C) narrowing
   D) both A and C

38. When choosing a topic, the speaker should *not* consider
   A) its appropriateness.
   B) whether the topic will make the audience laugh.
   C) whether the speaker can speak on the topic with enthusiasm.
   D) whether the speaker can offer a fresh perspective on the topic.

39. When narrowing a topic, the speaker should consider the
   A) time limit for speaking.
   B) speech purpose.
   C) amount of time available for research.
   D) all of the above.

40. The ______ speech purpose expresses both the topic and general speech purpose in action form and identifies the speaker's specific objectives.
   A) general
   B) initial
   C) specific
   D) ethical

41. A speech topic is considered unethical if the topic
   A) shows an audience how to perform illegal actions.
   B) provides audience members with information that may physically or psychologically harm them.
   C) is humiliating or degrading to the audience.
   D) involves any of the above.

42. The ______ concisely identifies, in a single idea, what the speech is about.
   A) topic
   B) thesis
   C) purpose
   D) claim

43. The ______ all emanate from the thesis.
   A) main points
   B) supporting points
   C) conclusion
   D) all of the above

FILL-IN-THE-BLANK QUESTIONS

44. To inform, to persuade, and to mark a special occasion are the three general speech ______.

45. A(n) ______ speech describes, defines, explains, or demonstrates something.

46. The general purpose of a(n) ______ speech is to effect some degree of change in the audience.

47. Controversial issues are good topic choices for a(n) ______ speech.

48. A speech of acceptance is a type of ______ speech.

49. If a speaker selects a topic that he or she is enthusiastic about and familiar with, the topic choice is based on ______ interests.

50. The problem-solving technique involving the spontaneous generation of ideas is termed ______.

51. Drawing a(n) ______ is a helpful way to visualize ideas for a speech.

52. When you ______ a speech topic, you focus on specific aspects of it to the exclusion of others.

53. Speech topic choices should always be guided by what is right, or ______ considerations.

54. The ______ statement is the theme or central idea of the speech.

55. The thesis should be ______ sentence(s) long.

ESSAY AND SHORT ANSWER QUESTIONS

56. Explain the major differences between informative and persuasive speech purposes.

57. List three topics suitable for a persuasive speech.

58. Discuss three types of special occasion speeches.

59. If you were assigned to write a speech based on your personal interests, what four topics would you consider for your speech?

60. Identify two current events or controversial issues appropriate for a classroom speech.

61. Identify two contemporary grassroots issues appropriate for a classroom speech.

62. Compare and contrast the brainstorming techniques of list making, word association, and topic mapping.

63. Discuss three things to consider when narrowing a speech topic.

64. How does the general speech purpose differ from the specific speech purpose?

65. Describe the components of the specific speech purpose.

66. Explain why a speaker should strive to be ethical when choosing a topic and delivering a speech.

67. Describe the similarities and differences between the thesis statement and the specific speech purpose.

68. Using an example, explain how a thesis statement makes a claim or assumption about a speech topic.

69. Explain why the nature of the thesis statement varies according to the speech purpose.

70. Choose a speech topic. Then write (a) a general speech purpose, (b) a specific speech purpose, and (c) a thesis statement.

71. How can a speaker make a thesis statement relevant to and motivating for the audience?

72. List three of the four criteria for formulating an effective thesis statement.

ANSWER KEY FOR CHAPTER 7

1. False (p. 94)
2. True (p. 94)
3. False (p. 95)
4. False (p. 95)
5. True (p. 95)
6. False (p. 95)
7. True (p. 95)
8. False (p. 95)
9. True (p. 95)
10. True (p. 95)
11. False (p. 96)
12. True (p. 97)
13. False (pp. 97–98)
14. False (p. 98)
15. True (p. 99)
16. False (p. 99)
17. True (p. 99)
18. False (p. 99)
19. True (p. 100)
20. True (pp. 101–102)
21. True (p. 102)
22. True (p. 103)
23. True (p. 103)
24. False (p. 104)
25. True (p. 104)
26. False (p. 104)
27. C (p. 94)
28. D (p. 94)
29. A (p. 95)
30. C (p. 95)
31. A (p. 96)
32. B (p. 97)
33. C (pp. 97–98)
34. C (p. 99)
35. D (p. 99)
36. B (pp. 99–100)
37. D (p. 100)
38. B (p. 101)
39. D (pp. 101–102)
40. C (p. 102)
41. D (p. 103)
42. B (p. 103)
43. D (p. 103)
44. purposes (p. 95)
45. informative (p. 95)
46. persuasive (p. 96)
47. persuasive (p. 96)
48. special occasion (p. 97)
49. personal (pp. 97-98)
50. brainstorming (p. 99)
51. topic map (p. 100)
52. narrow (p. 101)
53. ethical (p. 103)
54. thesis (p. 104)
55. One (p. 106)
56. (No answer, pp. 95–96)
57. (No answer, p. 96)
58. (No answer, p. 97)
59. (No answer, pp. 97–98)
60. (No answer, pp. 98–99)
61. (No answer, p. 99)
62. (No answer, p. 100)
63. (No answer, pp. 101–102)
64. (No answer, p. 102)
65. (No answer, p. 102)
66. (No answer, p. 103)
67. (No answer, p. 104)
68. (No answer, p. 104)
69. (No answer, pp. 104–105)
70. (No answer)
71. (No answer, p. 106)
72. (No answer, p. 106)

8 *Developing Supporting Material*

TRUE/FALSE QUESTIONS

1. Often, the most important element in a good speech is not the topic itself but how it is developed and supported.
2. Supporting material refers only to facts and statistics.
3. Alternating among different types of supporting material makes your presentation more confusing and thus less credible.
4. Mentioning the sources for your supporting material is equally important to the types of supporting material you select.
5. Examples in a speech weaken understanding by making ideas, items, or events less concrete.
6. Examples in a speech can be brief or extended.
7. One of the most powerful means of conveying a message is through a narrative, or story.
8. Hypothetical examples are effective for making a point about something that has already occurred.
9. Narratives tell tales that are either real or imaginary.
10. Sharing a personal experience is an effective type of supporting material, especially for ESL speakers.
11. Brief stories of interesting, humorous, or real-life incidents are called biographies.
12. Testimony comprises firsthand findings, eyewitness accounts, and opinions.
13. Lay testimony is testimony by nonexperts.
14. Most people require some type of evidence before they will accept a speaker's position or claims.
15. Facts are summarized data that demonstrate trends or show relationships.
16. *Statistics* are quantified evidence that summarizes complex information.
17. A *frequency* is the quantified portion of a whole.

18. Frequencies can be used to help the audience understand the magnitude of something, but cannot demonstrate trends.

19. The mean, median, and mode are all types of averages.

20. The median is the most frequently occurring score in a distribution.

21. In discussing the average income of a developing nation, the most accurate average would be the mean.

22. A source is likely to be more credible if it includes information about the methods used to generate the data and why the data was collected

MULTIPLE-CHOICE QUESTIONS

23. When used as supporting material in a speech, examples can
    A) illustrate.
    B) describe.
    C) clarify.
    D) do all of the above.

24. Effective examples for a speech may be all of the following *except*
    A) hypothetical.
    B) extended.
    C) factual.
    D) extraneous.

25. Which type of example offers a single illustration of a point?
    A) brief
    B) extended
    C) factual
    D) hypothetical

26. Which type of example offers a multifaceted illustration of a point?
    A) brief
    B) extended
    C) factual
    D) hypothetical

27. Legends, fairy tales, myths, and other stories are considered
    A) perspectives.
    B) narratives.
    C) testimonies.
    D) statistics.

28. Plot, characters, setting, and a time line are all essential to
    A) contextual examples.
    B) extended examples.
    C) storytelling.
    D) credibility.

29. Brief stories of interesting, humorous, or real-life incidents are called
    A) facts.
    B) testimony.
    C) statistics.
    D) anecdotes.

30. If a medical doctor gives cutting-edge information on the threat of high cholesterol, she is providing which type of supporting material?
    A) narrative material
    B) lay testimony
    C) expert testimony
    D) all of the above

31. The credibility of testimony can be evaluated by checking
    A) the reliability of the source.
    B) the timeliness of the information.
    C) both A and B.
    D) neither A nor B.

32. When citing testimony in a speech, the speaker should always
    A) supply the name and qualifications of the source.
    B) supply the inferential statistics related to the source.
    C) provide information about when, but not where, the testimony was offered.
    D) do none of the above.

33. Which type of average provides the center-most score in a distribution?
    A) mean
    B) mode
    C) median
    D) none of the above

34. What is a benefit of citing frequencies in speeches?
    A) They help listeners make comparisons between two or more categories.
    B) They help listeners understand the magnitude of something described.
    C) They demonstrate trends.
    D) All of the above.

35. A speaker selectively presenting only those statistics that buttress his or her point of view while ignoring competing data is said to be
    A) giving expert testimony.
    B) cherry-picking.
    C) speaking ethically.
    D) giving lay testimony.

FILL-IN-THE-BLANK QUESTIONS

36. ______ are a type of supporting material that aids audience understanding by making ideas, items, or events more concrete.

37. ______, which aid audience understanding, can be brief or extended and either factual or hypothetical.

38. ______ examples are effective for making a point about something that could happen in the future.

39. ______, or stories, tell tales that are either real or imaginary.

40. Brief stories of interesting, humorous, or real-life incidents are called ______.

41. Firsthand findings, eyewitness accounts, and opinions are types of ______.

42. ______ testimony includes findings, eyewitness accounts, or opinions by professionals who are qualified on a particular subject.

43. ______ testimony is testimony by nonexperts.

44. Documented occurrences, including actual events, dates, times, people involved, and places, are known as ______.

45. ______ is a count of the number of times something occurs.

46. The most frequently occurring score in a distribution is called the ______.

47. ______ represent a quantification of something at a given point in time.

48. ______ is selectively presenting only those statistics that support one's own point of view while ignoring competing data.

49. ______ is the quantified portion of a whole.

ESSAY AND SHORT ANSWER QUESTIONS

50. Explain why supporting material for a speech must be relevant, interesting, and accurate.

51. Provide an extended example for the topic "weight loss."

52. Why is a narrative such a powerful and compelling type of supporting material?

53. Explain why personal experiences make good narratives.

54. What is the difference between expert testimony and lay testimony?

55. How do facts differ from statistics?

56. When are statistics effective as supporting material in a speech?

57. Explain how speakers can ethically present statistics.

58. Explain how speakers can avoid presenting statistics as "absolute truth."

ANSWER KEY FOR CHAPTER 8

1. True (p. 115)
2. False (p. 115)
3. False (p. 115)
4. True (p. 115)
5. False (p. 116)
6. True (p. 116)
7. True (p. 117)
8. False (p. 117)
9. True (p. 117)
10. True (p. 119)
11. False (p. 119)
12. True (pp. 119–120)
13. True (p. 120)
14. True (p. 121)
15. False (p. 121)
16. True (p. 121)
17. False (p. 122)
18. False (p. 122)
19. True (p. 123)
20. False (p. 123)
21. False (p. 124)
22. True (p. 124)
23. D (p. 116)
24. D (pp. 116–117)
25. A (p. 116)
26. B (p. 116)
27. B (p. 117)
28. C (p. 118)
29. D (p. 119)
30. C (p. 120)
31. C (p. 120)
32. A (p. 120)
33. C (p. 123)
34. D (p. 122)
35. B (p. 127)
36. Examples (p. 116)
37. Examples (p. 116)
38. Hypothetical (p. 117)
39. Narratives (p. 117)
40. anecdotes (p. 119)
41. testimony (pp. 119–120)
42. Expert (p. 120)
43. Lay (p. 120)
44. Facts (p. 121)
45. Frequency (p. 122)
46. mode (p. 123)
47. Statistics (p. 126)
48. Cherry-picking (p. 127)
49. Percentage (p. 122)
50. (No answer, p. 115)
51. (No answer, p. 116)
52. (No answer, pp. 117–118)
53. (No answer, p. 118)
54. (No answer, p. 120)
55. (No answer, p. 121)
56. (No answer, pp. 122–124)
57. (No answer, pp. 124–127)
58. (No answer, pp. 126–127)

Locating Supporting Material 9

TRUE/FALSE QUESTIONS

1. Supporting material drawn from secondary research can include any source developed directly by the participants involved.
2. Original or firsthand research conducted by the speaker is primary research.
3. Two types of primary research are interviews and surveys.
4. The biggest pitfall in reviewing secondary research is wasting time by looking for information in the wrong places.
5. Different topics often require different research methods.
6. Some speech topics can be supported only through secondary research.
7. Secondary sources are those that appear only in print.
8. Information recorded by individuals other than actual participants in an event or study is termed *secondary research.*
9. Reference librarians are information specialists trained to help speakers search for information in the library but not on the Internet.
10. Libraries organize books and other holdings according to Library of Congress call numbers or Dewey decimal numbers.
11. Books explore topics superficially, not in depth.
12. A regularly published magazine or journal is called a *periodical.*
13. Some periodical databases are devoted to special topics.
14. WorldCat and ERIC are two of the many specialized databases available in libraries.
15. GPO publications are not good sources for government documents and statistics.
16. Encyclopedias, almanacs, and atlases are examples of reference works.
17. General encyclopedias delve deeply into one subject area.
18. The *Encyclopedia Britannica* is an example of a specialized encyclopedia.

19. Multicultural reference works are unavailable to researchers.

20. Almanacs may be general or specialized.

21. Almanacs and fact books are good places to find facts and statistics in support of a speech topic.

22. Biographical resources contain information about famous or noteworthy people.

23. Books of quotations and poetry collections are not examples of reference works.

24. An atlas is a collection of maps and text accompanied by charts and tables.

25. A speaker can gain considerably more insight on a topic by conducting an interview with an expert.

26. In an interview, vague questions help to reinforce the interviewer's agenda.

27. Leading questions in an interview encourage or force a particular response.

28. It is in the conclusion of the interview that you should pose your substantive questions.

29. Interviewers should focus on a list of prepared interview questions, and not permit the interviewee to introduce new topics.

30. Recording an interview helps the interviewer reconstruct exactly what was said during the interview.

31. Before recording an interview, it is not always necessary to obtain permission from the interviewee.

32. The interviewer may conduct an interview in either a casual or a professional manner.

33. Like interviews, surveys are useful tools for investigating audience attitudes.

34. Surveys of local people can serve as a source of additional speech support with direct relevance to audience members.

35. When copying quotations, statistics, or other information, the researcher is responsible for recording all information accurately.

36. Every piece of information you gather during your research should be cited by the speaker during the speech.

37. To assess the credibility of a publication, the speaker should check out the publisher and determine whether the source is reputable.

38. A speaker who cites statistics in a speech is not responsible for checking the reliability of the statistics.

39. Properly citing sources is central to conducting ethical research.

MULTIPLE-CHOICE QUESTIONS

40. When making an inventory of research needs, speakers should assess
    A) their own personal knowledge of the topic.
    B) the thesis statement's requirements.
    C) support material for the speech.
    D) all of the above.

41. Which of the following is *not* a type of secondary research?
    A) books
    B) newspapers
    C) surveys
    D) periodicals

42. The Declaration of Independence is an example of a ______ document.
    A) primary
    B) secondary
    C) tertiary
    D) chronicle

43. A regularly published magazine or journal is called a(n)
    A) annual.
    B) yearbook.
    C) periodical.
    D) guide.

44. *Newsweek* and *Time* are examples of
    A) government publications.
    B) periodicals.
    C) almanacs.
    D) biographical resources.

45. Which of the following is *not* a specialized database?
    A) ERIC
    B) PsycINFO
    C) Yahoo!
    D) WorldCat

46. GPO stands for
    A) Government Printing Office.
    B) Government Prototype Office.
    C) Government Production Office.
    D) Government Publishing Office.

47. The U.S. Government Printing Office publishes and distributes
    A) information produced by federal agencies.
    B) general encyclopedias.
    C) almanacs about other countries.
    D) information about the president.

48. Which type of reference work summarizes knowledge that is found in original form elsewhere?
A) encyclopedias
B) almanacs
C) biographical resources
D) poetry collections

49. An example of a multicultural reference work is
A) the *Dictionary of American Biography.*
B) the *Asian American Almanac.*
C) both A and B.
D) neither A nor B.

50. The *Biography Index* indexes biographical material from
A) periodicals, books, and obituaries.
B) only periodicals.
C) almanacs, periodicals, and obituaries.
D) none of the above.

51. An atlas is a collection of maps that can provide information on
A) human anatomy.
B) art history.
C) geography.
D) all of the above.

52. The vast world of information gathered by others is called ______ research.
A) primary
B) secondary
C) tertiary
D) questionnaire

53. Firsthand oral or written histories, diaries, and recordings of meetings and other events are examples of ______ sources.
A) primary
B) secondary
C) tertiary
D) chronicle

54. Effective interview questions are
A) often biased in some way.
B) made up spontaneously during the interview.
C) relevant to the purpose and topic of the speech.
D) all of the above.

55. Which of the following are types of primary research?
A) interviews and personal observations
B) almanacs
C) data on CD-ROMs
D) all of the above

56. Primary research does *not* include
A) information gathered by others.
B) personal interviews.
C) personal surveys.
D) all of the above.

57. Questions that don't lead the interviewer to a desired response are known as
    A) neutral questions.
    B) vague questions.
    C) loaded questions.
    D) closed questions.

58. A question designed to check that all important information has been discussed is called a(n)
    A) open question.
    B) secondary question.
    C) clearinghouse question.
    D) leading question.

59. To avoid inaccuracies in reporting from an interview, an interviewer can (with permission):
    A) repeat the interview multiple times.
    B) write down every single thing the interviewee says.
    C) tape-record the interview.
    D) do all of the above.

60. At the end of the interview, you should
    A) offer a brief, positive summary of important things you learned.
    B) exit as quickly as possible after thanking the interviewee.
    C) encourage the interviewee to contact you if he or she wishes to make corrections to any of his or her answers.
    D) offer a follow-up interview.

61. Surveys are a valuable source of support for topics related to the ______ of the people in a speaker's immediate environment.
    A) attitudes
    B) beliefs
    C) values
    D) all of the above

62. Material from books of ______ are often used by speakers in introductions and conclusions.
    A) myths
    B) quotations
    C) history
    D) biography

63. Three of the most commonly used systems of reference are
    A) APA, MLA, and CSE.
    B) APA, PHD, and MLA.
    C) APA, MLA, and IEEE.
    D) APA, MLA, and ERIC.

64. The APA system of reference, or style guide, stands for the
    A) Atlantic Pacific Association.
    B) American Psychological Association.
    C) Atlas Publication Association.
    D) American Publishing Association.

65. When citing source material in a bibliography, the speaker should include
    A) the author's biography.
    B) the title and year of publication.
    C) the ISBN number.
    D) all of the above.

66. When using a book as a source, the following element(s) should be recorded:
    A) title
    B) page number
    C) publisher
    D) all of the above

FILL-IN-THE-BLANK QUESTIONS

67. Information or research gathered by others is called ______ research.

68. When recording an interview, it is always necessary to obtain ______ to record from the interviewee.

69. A ______ is a searchable electronic resource in which at least some of the records contain the full text of articles.

70. Original or firsthand research conducted by the speaker is called ______ research.

71. Information recorded by individuals other than actual participants in an event or study is termed ______ research.

72. A(n) ______ is a searchable place in which information is stored and from which it can be retrieved.

73. Reference ______ are information specialists trained to help people search for information in the library

74. A regularly published magazine or journal is called a(n) ______.

75. Publications that are good sources for U.S. government documents and statistics are often produced by the ______.

76. Encyclopedias, almanacs, and atlases are examples of ______ works.

77. Encyclopedias that delve deeply into one subject area are known as ______ encyclopedias.

78. The *Encyclopedia Britannica* is an example of a(n) ______ encyclopedia.

79. Resources that contain information about famous or noteworthy people are termed ______ resources.

80. A collection of maps and text accompanied by charts and tables is called a(n) ______.

81. Two types of ______ research are interviews and surveys.

82. Interview questions that are phrased to reinforce the interviewer's agenda are known as ______ questions.

83. Questions in an interview that encourage or force a particular response from the interviewee are known as ______ questions.

84. ______ an interview helps the interviewer reconstruct exactly what was said during the interview.

85. Researchers use a ______ bibliography to keep track of bibliographic information as sources are reviewed.

ESSAY AND SHORT ANSWER QUESTIONS

86. Explain the difference between primary and secondary research.

87. When you are preparing a speech, why might books be valuable as supporting material?

88. How are newspapers and periodicals more beneficial than books?

89. Describe a speech in which a citation from a government publication would be useful.

90. Explain why books of quotations and poetry collections are good sources for speech introductions and conclusions.

91. Provide an example of a speech topic for which a speaker might consult an atlas.

92. Describe situations in which surveys and interviews are effective research tools for public speakers.

93. Give an example of a loaded interview question.

94. Give an example of a leading interview question.

95. Give an example of a vague interview question.

96. Why are clearly phrased interview questions advantageous to both the interviewer and the interviewee?

97. List three criteria for preparing valuable interview questions.

98. Why is it important for a speaker to get an interviewee's permission to audiotape or videotape the interview?

99. List two elements of professionalism in conducting an interview.

100. How can surveys effectively measure a local group's values or beliefs?

101. Name the main elements that a speaker should cite for a source in a biography.

102. Explain how to critically evaluate sources.

103. Discuss two ethical considerations in research.

ANSWER KEY FOR CHAPTER 9

1. False (p. 128)
2. True (p. 128)
3. True (p. 128)
4. True (p. 128)
5. True (p. 128)
6. True (p. 128)
7. False (p. 129)
8. True (p. 129)
9. False (p. 130)
10. True (p. 130)
11. False (p. 130)
12. True (p. 130)
13. True (p. 131)
14. True (p. 131)
15. False (p. 132)
16. True (p. 132)
17. False (p. 132)
18. False (p. 132)
19. False (p. 133)
20. True (p. 133)
21. True (p. 133)
22. True (p. 134)
23. False (p. 134)
24. True (p. 134)
25. True (p. 135)
26. False (p. 135)
27. True (p. 135)
28. False (p. 136)
29. False (p. 136)
30. True (p. 137)
31. False (p. 137)
32. False (p. 137)
33. True (p. 138)
34. True (p. 138)
35. True (p. 138)
36. False (p. 138)
37. True (p. 141)
38. False (p. 146)
39. True (p. 146)
40. D (p. 129)
41. C (p. 129)
42. A (p. 135)
43. C (p. 130)
44. B (p. 131)
45. C (p. 131)
46. A (p. 132)
47. A (p. 132)
48. A (p. 132)
49. B (p. 133)
50. A (p. 134)
51. D (p. 134)
52. A (p. 135)
53. A (p. 135)
54. C (p. 135)
55. A (p. 135)
56. A (p. 135)
57. A (p. 135)
58. C (p. 136)
59. C (p. 137)
60. A (p. 137)
61. D (p. 138)
62. B (p. 134)
63. A (p. 138)
64. B (p. 138)
65. B (p. 139)
66. D (p. 142)
67. secondary (p. 129)
68. permission (p. 137)
69. full-text database (p. 129)
70. primary (p. 128)
71. secondary (p. 129)
72. database (p. 129)
73. librarians (p. 130)
74. periodical (p. 130)
75. GPO (p. 132)
76. reference (p. 132)
77. specialized (p. 132)
78. general (p. 132)
79. biographical (p. 134)
80. atlas (p.134)
81. primary (p. 135)
82. loaded (p. 135)
83. leading (p. 135)
84. Recording (p. 137)
85. working (p.138)
86. (No answer, p. 128)
87. (No answer, p. 130)
88. (No answer, pp. 130–131)
89. (No answer, p. 132)
90. (No answer, p. 134)
91. (No answer, p. 134)
92. (No answer, pp. 135–138)
93. (No answer, p. 135)
94. (No answer, p. 135)
95. (No answer, p. 135)
96. (No answer, p. 135)
97. (No answer, p. 135)
98. (No answer, p. 137)
99. (No answer, pp. 137–138)
100. (No answer, p. 138)
101. (No answer, p. 139)
102. (No answer, pp. 141–144)
103. (No answer, p. 141)

10 *Using the Internet to Support Your Speech*

TRUE/FALSE QUESTIONS

1. The World Wide Web contains text, images, sound, and video.
2. The most frequently used portion of the Internet is e-mail.
3. Library holdings are built through a careful, deliberate selection by professionals.
4. Both libraries and the Internet classify and order their resources according to well-defined standards.
5. E-mail, chat rooms, listservs, and newsgroups are not helpful resources when searching the Internet for supporting material for a speech.
6. All Web documents are current.
7. Newsgroups contain e-mail messages on specific topics, and the messages are exchanged among subscribers.
8. The term *real-time communication* refers to electronic forums or "rooms" for conversing with others and attending online classes and conferences.
9. A government-sponsored site is no more credible than other primary materials.
10. One way to evaluate the credibility of a Web site is to look for the last date the site was modified or updated.
11. The domain of a Web address is the suffix at the end of the address that indicates the nature of the site.
12. A tilde (~) in a Web address usually indicates that it is a commercial page.
13. The mission statement or "About Us" link usually tells a great deal about the nature of a particular Web site and the organization.
14. It is not necessary to check that the site credits its sources and that those sources are credible.
15. The terms *misinformation* and *disinformation* are synonymous.

16. Propaganda aims to instill a particular attitude.
17. The word *misinformation* always refers to something that is not true.
18. Meaningful speeches are based on sound information rather than on misinformation.
19. Propaganda is always based on false information.
20. Information, propaganda, misinformation, and disinformation are four criteria to consider when evaluating Internet sources.
21. A search engine automatically retrieves documents that match keywords or phrases entered by the user.
22. All Internet search engines use the same criteria to determine search relevance.
23. Two types of search engines are individual and meta-search.
24. Search engines that use paid placement scan a variety of individual search engines simultaneously.
25. MetaCrawler and Dogpile are examples of meta-search engines.
26. Individual search engines compile their own databases of Web pages.
27. Most search engines do not order search results according to relevance.
28. Information found on Internet search engines and subject directories is complete and infallible.
29. 24HourScholar.com and GoogleScholar.com are specialized search engines.
30. Subject directories are not useful for finding and narrowing a speech topic.
31. Similar to some search engines, subject directories compile databases of their own.
32. Subject directories can be searched by using keywords or phrases.
33. Both search engines and subject directories offer valuable help in locating supporting materials for a speech.
34. A subject directory is a good place to start brainstorming for information on a speech topic.
35. A *gateway* is a subject directory that has been reviewed by an expert.
36. Most universities and city libraries offer library gateways in the form of their library's home page.

37. The *invisible web* is a portion of the Web that general search engines fail to find.

38. A password is not usually required to access databases on a library gateway.

39. Virtual libraries exist on the Internet.

40. Researchers should rely on a single large search engine when seeking speech sources.

41. Library gateways and specialty search engines are not good sources of direct links to the invisible Web.

42. When you use search tools on the Internet, quotation marks help you locate exact phrases.

43. *Boolean operators* are words placed between keywords in a search that specify how the keywords are related.

44. Using the word OR in an Internet search restricts the search by excluding specific terms from the results.

45. The plus and minus signs are the equivalent of the Boolean operators AND and NOT.

46. The style of documenting Internet sources remains constant across disciplines.

47. A retrieval date statement is required for most referencing styles

48. The fees that companies pay for a guaranteed higher ranking within search results are called *paid inclusion.*

49. When documenting Internet sources, you do not need to include the URL.

MULTIPLE-CHOICE QUESTIONS

50. Hyperlinks are
    A) graphics-rich environments of electronic pages containing text, graphics, sound, and video.
    B) connections that link individual pieces of information or entire sites to other pieces of information or sites.
    C) personal messages and attached files.
    D) e-mail messages on specific topics that are exchanged among subscribers.

51. One benefit of using the Web is that
    A) all relevant information is available on it.
    B) offerings are selected by trained professionals.
    C) sources have a potential for currency.
    D) all of the above.

52. Electronic forums or "rooms" for conversing with others and attending online classes are examples of
A) newsgroups.
B) .listservs.
C) Weblogs.
D) real-time communication.

53. The key to a productive search in cyberspace depends on
A) a well-prepared research strategy.
B) an understanding of information available on the Internet.
C) a basic grasp of how to use Internet search tools.
D) all of the above.

54. Which of the following domain suffixes indicates a nonprofit group?
A) .org
B) .net
C) .com
D) .gov

55. ______ refers to something that is not true.
A) Information
B) Misinformation
C) Propaganda
D) Disinformation

56. To efficiently locate information on the Internet for a speech, the speaker should be familiar with the function of
A) search engines and subject directories.
B) library gateways and specialized databases.
C) both A and B.
D) neither A nor B.

57. *Spiders, bots,* and *crawlers* are all common names for
A) software programs used by Internet search engines.
B) Web discussion forums.
C) Web-based newsgroups.
D) none of the above.

58. Which of the following is an example of a search engine on the Internet?
A) Yahoo!
B) Google
C) MSN Search
D) all of the above

59. Meta-search engines
A) scan a variety of individual search engines simultaneously.
B) compile their own databases of Web pages.
C) provide a variety of unpaid listings.
D) are always recommended by libraries.

60. Search engines
A) index the contents of the Web.
B) seldom consider relevance when ranking search results.
C) can only search for exact matches rather than keywords or phrases.
D) require passwords for access

61. Which types of search engines are devoted entirely to one topic?
    A) specialized search engines
    B) subject directories
    C) meta-search engines
    D) individual search engines

62. Which of the following is *not* an important distinction to consider when evaluating Internet sources?
    A) misinformation
    B) propaganda
    C) information
    D) reification

63. A subject directory
    A) is also known as a human directory.
    B) is a searchable database of Web sites organized by categories.
    C) does not compile databases of its own.
    D) all of the above.

64. A searchable database that allows a researcher to "drill down" into a topic is called a
    A) library portal.
    B) subject directory.
    C) humansearch.
    D) Commstar.

65. If a speaker is brainstorming ideas online and wants to survey what is available on a particular speech topic, she or he should begin by selecting a
    A) library catalog.
    B) gateway.
    C) subject directory.
    D) search engine.

66. When looking for a specific page within a site, a researcher should use a
    A) subject directory
    B) search engine
    C) weblog
    D) listserv

67. Fees paid to search engines that guarantee companies a higher ranking are called
    A) crawler-based placement
    B) paid placement
    C) individual fees
    D) specialized fees

68. The most effective way to find and narrow a topic online is to use
    A) search engines.
    B) subject directories.
    C) neither A nor B.
    D) both A and B.

69. A subject directory that has been reviewed by an expert is called a
    A) library catalog.
    B) gateway.
    C) subject directory.
    D) search engine.

70. The portion of the Web that general search engines fail to find is called the
    A) imperceptible Web.
    B) unseen Web.
    C) undetectable Web.
    D) invisible Web.

71. AND, OR, and NOT are examples of
    A) bookmark tools.
    B) Boolean operators.
    C) domains.
    D) library gateways.

72. Which of the following words expands an online search?
    A) AND
    B) OR
    C) NOT
    D) PLUS

73. In an online search, the plus (+) and minus (–) signs are equivalent to the Boolean operator(s)
    A) AND.
    B) OR.
    C) PLUS and NOT.
    D) AND and NOT.

74. Which of the following are the most widely used formats for documenting sources?
    A) APA, MLA, and Chicago
    B) APA, MCB, and IEEE
    C) APA, IEEE, and PHD
    D) APA, CBE, and MCB

FILL-IN-THE-BLANK QUESTIONS

75. The distinguishing feature of the Web is ______—connections that link individual pieces of information and/or entire sites.

76. The most frequently used portion of the Internet is the ______.

77. ______ are connections that link individual pieces of information or sites to other pieces of information or sites on the Web.

78. ______ are Web pages that contain a log of a writer's thoughts.

79. ______ contain e-mail messages on specific topics, which are exchanged among subscribers.

80. The ______ of a Web address is the suffix at the end of the address that indicates the nature of the site.

81. A(n) ______, or (~), in a Web address usually indicates that it is a personal page.

82. A military web address domain is ______.

83. ______ directories are useful for finding and narrowing a speech topic.

84. Search engines that scan individual search engines simultaneously but do not compile their own databases are known as ______.

85. Most search engines rank search results according to ______.

86. A ______ directory is a searchable database of Web sites that have been organized into categories.

87. A(n) ______ directory is a good place to start brainstorming for information on a speech topic.

88. A(n) ______ is a subject directory that contains research and reference materials that have been reviewed by an expert.

89. A(n) ______ is usually required for access to databases on a library gateway.

90. Libraries that exist only on the Internet are known as ______ libraries.

91. The ______ Web is the portion of the Web that general search engines fail to find.

92. A search that narrows results beyond basic options by analyzing attributes common to all Web pages is ______ searching.

93. ______ are words placed between keywords in a search that specify how the keywords are related.

94. The minus sign is the equivalent of the Boolean operator ______.

ESSAY AND SHORT ANSWER QUESTIONS

95. Describe the main components of the Internet, how they differ, and what they have to offer.

96. Discuss the four important distinctions to consider when evaluating Internet sources.

97. Describe three ways in which a student can critically evaluate Internet sources.

98. What is a domain, and how does it help identify a Web address? Give two examples of a domain.

99. Explain the difference between an individual search engine and a meta-search engine.

100. Describe and provide an example of a specialized search engine.

101. Define *subject directory* and explain its use.

102. When is a subject directory more beneficial to research than a search engine?

103. How is a gateway distinguished from a library gateway?

104. What is the invisible Web?

105. Describe the steps in creating an online search strategy.

106. List three search commands and explain how each command enhances online results.

107. Explain how to establish Internet source credibility in a speech.

108. List four pieces of information that must be included when documenting Internet sources.

ANSWER KEY FOR CHAPTER 10

1. True (p. 147)
2. False (p. 147)
3. True (p. 147)
4. False (p. 147)
5. False (p. 147)
6. False (p. 148)
7. False (p. 148)
8. True (p. 148)
9. False (p. 150)
10. True (p. 150)
11. True (p. 150)
12. False (p. 150)
13. True (p. 150)
14. False (p. 150)
15. False (p. 152)
16. True (p. 152)
17. True (p. 152)
18. True (p. 152)
19. False (p. 152)
20. True (p. 152)
21. True (p. 153)
22. False (p. 153)
23. True (p. 153)
24. False (p. 153)
25. True (p. 153)
26. True (p. 153)
27. False (p. 153)
28. False (pp. 153–156)
29. True (p. 154)
30. False (p. 154)
31. False (p. 154)
32. True (p. 155)
33. True (p. 155)
34. True (p. 156)
35. True (p. 157)
36. True (p. 157)
37. True (p. 157)
38. False (p. 157)
39. True (p. 157)
40. False (p. 157)
41. False (p. 157)
42. True (p. 159)
43. True (p. 159)
44. False (p. 159)
45. True (p. 159)
46. False (p. 164)
47. True (p. 164)
48. False (p. 156)
49. False (p. 164)
50. B (p. 147)
51. C (p. 148)
52. D (p. 148)
53. D (p. 147)
54. A (p. 150)
55. B (p. 152)
56. C (p. 153)
57. A (p. 153)
58. D (p. 153)
59. A (p. 153)
60. A (p. 153)
61. A (p. 154)
62. D (p. 152)
63. B (p. 154)
64. B (p. 154)
65. C (p. 156)
66. B (p. 156)
67. B (p. 156)
68. B (p. 156)
69. B (p. 157)
70. D (p. 159)
71. B (p. 159)
72. B (p. 159)
73. D (p. 150)
74. A (p. 164)
75. hyperlinks (p. 147)
76. World Wide Web (p. 147)
77. Hyperlinks (p. 147)
78. Weblogs (p. 148)
79. Listservs (p. 148)
80. domain (p. 150)
81. tilde (p. 150)
82. .mil (p. 150)
83. Subject (p. 156)
84. meta-search engines (p. 153)
85. relevance (p. 153)
86. subject (p. 154)
87. subject (p. 156)
88. gateway (p. 157)
89. password or pin number (p. 157)
90. virtual (p. 157)
91. invisible (p. 157)
92. field (p. 159)
93. Boolean operators (p. 159)
94. NOT (p. 159)
95. (No answer, pp. 147–149)
96. (No answer, p. 150)
97. (No answer, p. 149)
98. (No answer, p. 152)
99. (No answer, p. 153)
100. (No answer, p. 154)
101. (No answer, pp. 154–155)
102. (No answer, pp. 155–156)
103. (No answer, p. 157)
104. (No answer, p. 157)
105. (No answer, pp. 158–160)
106. (No answer, p. 159)
107. (No answer, p. 161)
108. (No answer, p. 164)

11 *Organizing the Speech*

TRUE/FALSE QUESTIONS

1. Outlining cannot help you check for logical inconsistencies in the placement of speech points.
2. Listeners' understanding of a speech is directly linked to how well it is organized.
3. The organization of a speech does not influence the audience's perception of speaker credibility.
4. The structure of a speech is composed of three main parts: an introduction, a body, and a conclusion.
5. The body of a speech establishes the speech purpose and shows its relevance to the audience.
6. The introduction of a speech tells listeners where they are going.
7. Main points express the key ideas and major themes of the speech.
8. The first step in creating main points is to identify the central ideas and themes of the speech.
9. The thesis statement expresses the goal of the speech, whereas the specific purpose expresses the theme or central idea of the speech.
10. Research shows that audiences can comfortably take in between eight and ten main points.
11. Listeners have better recall of the main points made at the beginning and at the end of a speech than of those made in between.
12. To help the audience remember what you say, use as few main points as possible.
13. A main point should not introduce more than two ideas.
14. Whenever possible, main points should be stated in parallel form.
15. Each main point should be expressed as an interrogative sentence.
16. Presenting each main point as a declarative statement emphasizes the point and makes it stand out from the others.

17. Supporting points represent the supporting material or evidence that a speaker has gathered to justify the main points.

18. Listeners respond most favorably to a variety of supporting materials derived from a single source to illustrate each main point.

19. In an outline, supporting points appear in a superordinate position to the main points.

20. The most common outline format is the Roman numeral outline.

21. In a Roman numeral outline, third-level points are enumerated with Arabic numerals.

22. In an outline, indentation indicates different levels of points.

23. Indentations in an outline enhance the speaker's recollection of points and make it easy for the speaker to follow the outline as he or she speaks.

24. Whether one is creating a painting, an essay, a musical composition, or a speech, certain principles of good form apply.

25. A well-organized speech is characterized by unity, coherence, and balance.

26. *Coherence* refers to a speech containing only those points that are implied by the purpose and thesis statements.

27. In speeches that have unity, each point focuses on a single idea.

28. *Unity* refers to clarity and logical consistency.

29. The speech body should follow logically from the introduction, and the conclusion should follow logically from the body.

30. Ideas that are coordinate are given equal weight.

31. In an outline, subordinate points are indicated by their parallel alignment, and coordinate points are indicated by their indentation below the more important points.

32. In an outline, main point II is subordinate to main point I, and subpoint A is coordinate to main point I.

33. The principle of balance suggests that appropriate emphasis or weight be given to each part of the speech relative to the other parts and to the theme.

34. The introduction of a speech should always be the longest part.

35. Assigning each main point at least two supporting points is one aspect of balance.

36. Words, phrases, or sentences that tie the speech ideas together and enable the speaker to move smoothly from one point to the next are called *transitions.*

37. The words *similarly, however,* and *finally* are examples of transitional words and phrases.

38. In moving between supporting points, conjunctions or phrases such as *next* and *finally, let's consider* are effective.

39. Transitions may be stated as rhetorical questions, but they should not be stated in restate-forecast form.

40. A type of transition that tells the audience what to expect next is called the *external preview.*

41. The external preview is often used in speech introductions.

42. Within the body itself, internal previews can be used to preview an ensuing main point.

43. The internal summary is the same as the internal preview.

44. Internal summaries are often used in speech conclusions.

MULTIPLE-CHOICE QUESTIONS

45. The speech conclusion brings closure to the speech by
    A) restating the purpose.
    B) reiterating why the purpose is relevant to the audience.
    C) leaving audience members with something to think about.
    D) doing all of the above.

46. The body of a speech consists of
    A) thesis statements and introductions.
    B) main points, supporting points, and transitions.
    C) specific purpose statements and internal summaries.
    D) all of the above.

47. Which of the following expresses the speech goal?
    A) specific speech purpose
    B) thesis statement
    C) main points
    D) all of the above

48. Which of the following helps to determine the number of main points for a speech?
    A) the topic
    B) the amount of material to be covered
    C) the length of the speech
    D) all of the above

49. Research indicates that audiences prefer speeches that contain ______ main points.
A) one to two
B) two to seven
C) five to ten
D) at least six

50. Facts, statistics, testimonies, and narratives are all examples of
A) main points.
B) transitions.
C) supporting material.
D) none of the above.

51. The speaker should express each main point as a(n) ______ sentence.
A) interrogative
B) declarative
C) directive
D) exclamatory

52. A well-organized speech is characterized by
A) unity, coherence, and balance.
B) unity, coordination, and balance.
C) unity, subordination, and coherence.
D) unity, coordination, and subordination.

53. Which of the following is a common mistake on the part of an inexperienced speaker?
A) giving overly lengthy coverage to one point and insufficient attention to others
B) giving scanty evidence in the body of the speech after presenting an impressive introduction
C) jumping right into the speech without properly introducing the topic
D) all of the above

54. Effective transitions move listeners from
A) one main point to the next.
B) a main point to a supporting point.
C) one supporting point to another supporting point.
D) all of the above.

55. What type of transition is the following sentence? *Now that we have established a need for the blood-bank drive, let's look at how the blood drive will benefit our community.*
A) rhetorical question
B) restate-forecast
C) internal preview
D) external preview

56. Which type of transition tells the audience what to expect next?
A) rhetorical question
B) restate-forecast
C) internal preview
D) external preview

57. Internal summaries are often used in the speech
A) introduction.
B) body.
C) conclusion.
D) transitions.

FILL-IN-THE-BLANK QUESTIONS

58. The ______ of a speech establishes the speech purpose and shows its relevance to the audience.

59. ______ points express the key ideas and major themes of the speech.

60. The ______ expresses the goal of the speech.

61. The ______ expresses the theme or central idea of the speech.

62. A main point should not introduce more than ______ idea(s).

63. Each main point should be expressed in the form of a(n) ______ sentence.

64. ______ points represent the supporting material or evidence that a speaker has gathered.

65. ______ is the most common outline format.

66. In an outline, changes in numbering and ______ indicate different levels of points.

67. A well-organized speech is characterized by unity, ______, and balance.

68. A speech exhibits ______ when it contains only those points that are implied by the purpose and thesis statements.

69. Ideas that are ______ are given equal weight.

70. Points in an outline that are indicated by their parallel alignment are known as ______ points.

71. Points in an outline that are indicated by their indentation below the more important points are known as ______ points.

72. The principle of ______ suggests that appropriate emphasis or weight be given to each part of the speech relative to the other parts and to the theme.

73. The ______ of a speech should always be the longest part.

74. Assigning each main point at least two supporting points is one aspect of ______.

75. Words, phrases, or sentences that tie the speech ideas together and enable the speaker to move smoothly from one point to the next are called ______.

76. A type of transition that tells the audience what to expect next and is often used in introductions is the ______.

77. ______ summaries are a type of transition often used in speech conclusions.

ESSAY AND SHORT ANSWER QUESTIONS

78. Explain how the specific purpose and thesis statements serve as guideposts in creating main points.

79. Why should a speaker adhere to the rule of using only two to seven main points?

80. Give two reasons why each main point in an outline should be presented as a declarative statement.

81. Within an outline, how can a speaker ensure that supporting points are subordinate to the main points?

82. Discuss why the body of the speech should be the longest part.

83. Why is it important to make the speech introduction and conclusion roughly the same length?

84. Define *unity, coherence,* and *balance* and give an example of each.

85. Define and give an example of an *internal preview.*

86. How do internal summaries help listeners review what the speaker said?

ANSWER KEY FOR CHAPTER 11

1. False (p. 171)
2. True (p. 171)
3. False (p. 171)
4. True (p. 172)
5. False (p. 172)
6. True (p. 172)
7. True (p. 173)
8. True (p. 173)
9. False (p. 173)
10. False (p. 174)
11. True (p. 174)
12. True (p. 174)
13. False (p. 175)
14. True (p. 175)
15. False (p. 176)
16. True (p. 176)
17. True (p. 176)
18. False (p. 176)
19. False (p. 177)
20. True (p. 177)
21. True (p. 177)
22. True (p. 178)
23. True (p. 178)
24. True (p. 178)
25. True (pp. 178–179)
26. False (p. 178)
27. True (p. 178)
28. False (p. 178)
29. True (p. 179)
30. True (p. 179)
31. False (p. 179)
32. False (p. 179)
33. True (p. 179)
34. False (p. 179)
35. True (pp. 179–180)
36. True (p. 180)
37. True (p. 181)
38. True (p. 182)
39. False (p. 182)
40. False (p. 182)
41. False (p. 182)
42. True (p. 182)
43. False (p. 182)
44. True (p. 182)
45. D (p. 172)
46. B (p. 172)
47. A (p. 173)
48. D (p. 173)
49. B (p. 174)
50. C (p. 176)
51. B (p. 176)
52. A (p. 178)
53. D (p. 179)
54. D (pp. 180–182)
55. B (p. 182)
56. C (p. 182)
57. C (p. 182)
58. introduction (p. 172)
59. Main (p. 173)
60. specific purpose statement (p. 173)
61. thesis statement (p. 173)
62. one (p. 175)
63. declarative (p. 176)
64. Supporting (p. 176)
65. Roman numeral (p. 177)
66. indentation (p. 177)
67. coherence (p. 178)
68. unity (p. 178)
69. coordinate (p. 179)
70. coordinate (p. 179)
71. subordinate (p. 179)
72. balance (p. 179)
73. body (p. 179)
74. balance (pp. 179–180)
75. transitions (p. 180)
76. internal preview (p. 182)
77. Internal (p. 182)
78. (No answer, p. 173)
79. (No answer, p. 174)
80. (No answer, p. 176)
81. (No answer, p. 179)
82. (No answer, p. 179)
83. (No answer, p. 179)
84. (No answer, pp. 178–179)
85. (No answer, p. 182)
86. (No answer, p. 182)

Types of Organizational Arrangements 12

TRUE/FALSE QUESTIONS

1. Some common organizational arrangements for public speeches are topical, spatial, causal, and problem-solution.
2. Organization should be driven by what is most effective for the particular rhetorical situation.
3. Your subpoints should always follow the organizational pattern selected for your main points.
4. A topical pattern of arrangement is most appropriate when each main point is of relatively equal importance.
5. In a topical pattern, points can be arranged in any order without negatively affecting each other or the speech purpose.
6. Chronological arrangements give the speaker the greatest freedom of all organizational arrangements to structure main points according to the audience's interests and the circumstances of the occasion.
7. A chronological pattern of arrangement follows the natural sequential order of the main points.
8. A speech describing a series of events in the development of a new idea calls for a spatial pattern of arrangement.
9. Topics that involve time lines or a series of sequential steps require the chronological pattern of arrangement.
10. The spatial pattern describes the physical arrangement of a place, scene, or object.
11. The causal pattern relates a cause to its effects.
12. It is never appropriate to present the effect first and the causes subsequently in the causal pattern.
13. Speakers usually select a causal arrangement when the general speech purpose is to persuade.

14. The problem-solution pattern of arrangement may have more than two main points.

15. The function of the problem-solution pattern is to demonstrate the nature and significance of a problem and to provide justification for a proposed solution.

16. The chronological pattern of arrangement assumes a largely Asian orientation to time.

17. Certain organizational formats may be better suited to certain cultures.

MULTIPLE-CHOICE QUESTIONS

18. To stress natural divisions in a topic, a speaker should use which pattern of arrangement?
A) topical
B) chronological
C) spatial
D) causal

19. To describe a series of developments in time or a set of actions that occur sequentially, a speaker should use which pattern of arrangement?
A) topical
B) chronological
C) spatial
D) causal

20. To explain the physical arrangement of a place, a scene, or an object, a speaker should use which pattern of arrangement?
A) topical
B) chronological
C) spatial
D) causal

21. To discuss a topic in terms of its underlying causes, a speaker should use which pattern of arrangement?
A) topical
B) chronological
C) causal
D) circle

22. To demonstrate the nature and significance of a problem and provide justification for a proposed solution, a speaker should use which pattern of arrangement?
A) topical
B) chronological
C) causal
D) problem-solution

23. If a speech consists of a story or series of short stories, which pattern of organization is the speaker using?
A) chronological
B) spatial
C) narrative
D) problem-solution

FILL-IN-THE-BLANK QUESTIONS

24. In the ______ pattern of arrangement, the speaker develops one idea, which leads to another, which leads to a third, and so forth.

25. A(n) ______ pattern of arrangement is most appropriate when each main point is of relatively equal importance.

26. In a(n) ______ pattern, points can be arranged in any order without negatively affecting each other or the speech purpose.

27. The ______ pattern of arrangement gives the speaker the greatest freedom to structure main points according to the audience's interests and the circumstances of the occasion.

28. A(n) ______ pattern of arrangement follows the natural sequential order of the main points.

29. A speech describing a series of events in the development of a new idea calls for a ______ pattern of arrangement.

30. Topics that involve time lines or a series of sequential steps require the ______ pattern of arrangement.

31. The ______ pattern describes the physical arrangement of a place, scene, or object.

32. The ______ pattern relates a cause to its effects.

33. A speech consisting of characters, settings, a plot, and imagery uses a ______ pattern.

34. The function of the ______ pattern is to demonstrate the nature and significance of a problem and to provide justification for a proposed solution.

35. The ______ pattern involves conveying ideas through the medium of a story.

ESSAY AND SHORT ANSWER QUESTIONS

36. How can a speaker best decide how to arrange main points in a speech?

37. When is the chronological pattern of arrangement appropriate for a speech?

38. Give an example of the spatial pattern of arrangement.

39. Explain the difference between the causal and the problem-solution patterns of arrangement.

40. Why is it important for the speaker to match the organizational pattern to the audience?

41. Provide main points for a speech on the topic of "The Internet" using a causal pattern of arrangement.

42. Provide main points using a chronological pattern of arrangement for a speech on the topic of "American Wars."

43. Provide main points using a spatial pattern of arrangement for a speech on the topic of "The Olympic Games."

44. Explain and provide an example of how a speech can use more than one organizational pattern.

ANSWER KEY FOR CHAPTER 12

1. True (p. 184)
2. True (p. 184)
3. False (p. 184)
4. True (p. 184)
5. True (p. 185)
6. False (p. 186)
7. True (p. 186)
8. False (p. 186)
9. True (p. 186)
10. True (p. 186)
11. True (p. 187)
12. False (p. 188)
13. False (p. 188)
14. True (p. 189)
15. True (p. 188)
16. False (p. 191)
17. True (p. 191)
18. A (p. 185)
19. B (p. 185)
20. C (p. 185)
21. C (p. 185)
22. D (p. 185)
23. C (p. 189)
24. circular (p. 190)
25. topical (p. 184)
26. topical (p. 185)
27. topical (p. 185)
28. chronological (p. 186)
29. chronological (p. 186)
30. chronological (p. 186)
31. spatial (p. 186)
32. causal (p. 187)
33. narrative (p. 189)
34. problem-solution (p. 188)
35. narrative (p. 189)
36. (No answer, p. 184)
37. (No answer, p. 186)
38. (No answer, p. 186)
39. (No answer, pp. 187–189)
40. (No answer, p. 191)
41. (No answer, p. 185)
42. (No answer, p. 186)
43. (No answer, p. 186)
44. (No answer, p. 186)

13 *Outlining the Speech*

TRUE/FALSE QUESTIONS

1. When developing a speech, a speaker should create two separate outlines: a working outline and a delivery outline.
2. Sentence outlines are generally used for working outlines.
3. Outlines can help with brainstorming as well as presentation of a speech.
4. Outlines assist in examining the underlying logic of a speech.
5. The purpose of a speaking outline is to refine and finalize the specific purpose statement, firm up and organize main points, and develop supporting points to substantiate them.
6. Working outlines are meant to be changed as a speaker works through the information and ideas collected for a speech.
7. Once the speaking outline is complete, the speaker should transfer its ideas to the working outline.
8. Speeches may be outlined in complete sentences, phrases, or key words.
9. Sentence outlines represent the full text of the speech.
10. Generally, sentence outlines are used for speaking outlines.
11. A sentence outline is effective for delivering a speech when the speech topic is highly controversial or emotional.
12. A phrase outline is effective when the material is highly technical and exact sentence structure is critical.
13. The first step in organizing and outlining a speech is to create the main points.
14. Speaking professionals recommend that the actual speaking outline be prepared using a full-sentence format.
15. Writing an outline in full sentences can build speaker confidence.
16. In the working outline, each section of the speech (introduction, body, and conclusion) should be labeled.

17. A phrase outline is the briefest form of outline.

18. A phrase outline uses a partial construction of the sentence form of each point.

19. The type of outline selected affects how well the speaker delivers the speech.

20. Eye contact is not very important to the successful delivery of a speech.

21. Phrase outlines or key-word outlines are recommended over sentence outlines in the delivery of most speeches.

22. Phrase outlines are the preferred format for speaking outlines.

23. Extemporaneous speeches are carefully planned and practiced in advance and are then delivered from a key-word or phrase outline.

24. The full-sentence outline restricts eye contact with the audience.

25. The speaking outline should be prepared on full sheets of paper.

26. In the speaking outline, the introduction and conclusion are among the main points.

27. The speech introduction and conclusion should be placed on separate notecards.

28. A speaking outline should contain brief parenthetical notes indicating transitions, sources to cite, and presentation aids.

29. Practice can significantly improve the delivery of a speech.

MULTIPLE-CHOICE QUESTIONS

30. Which of the following outlines is an in-process document to be revised and rearranged until the speaker is satisfied with it?
    A) working
    B) speaking
    C) sentence
    D) key-word

31. Which of the following outlines should be prepared in a full-sentence format?
    A) working
    B) speaking
    C) phrase
    D) key-word

32. Which of the following outlines uses a partial construction of the sentence form of each point?
    A) working
    B) speaking
    C) sentence
    D) phrase

33. Which of the following outlines uses a few words associated with each specific point?
    A) working
    B) speaking
    C) key-word
    D) phrase

34. Which of the following outlines offers the most protection against memory lapses?
    A) working
    B) speaking
    C) key-word
    D) sentence

35. Which type of outline is easiest to handle and follow if the speaker is well rehearsed?
    A) working
    B) speaking
    C) key-word
    D) none of the above

36. The speaking outline should
    A) be written on small notecards.
    B) be written in large print.
    C) include transitions.
    D) all of the above.

37. The final step in creating a working outline is to
    A) label each speech part.
    B) assign the speech a title.
    C) prepare a list of sources.
    D) label and write out transitions.

FILL-IN-THE-BLANK QUESTIONS

38. When developing a speech, the speaker should create two separate outlines: a ______ outline and a ______ outline.

39. Written structures known as ______ are critical to organizing a speech.

40. The purpose of the ______ outline is to refine and finalize the specific purpose statement, firm up and organize main points, and develop supporting points to substantiate them.

41. A type of outline that is meant to be changed as the speaker works through the information and ideas for a speech is called a ______ outline.

42. Once the working outline is complete, the speaker should transfer its ideas to the ______ outline.

43. Speeches may be outlined in complete sentences, key words, or ______.

44. A type of outline that represents the full text of the speech is known as a ______ outline.

45. ______ outlines permit more eye contact and greater freedom of movement than any other outline format.

46. A(n) ______ outline is effective for an inexperienced speaker.

47. A(n) ______ outline is effective when the material is highly technical and exact sentence structure is critical.

48. The first step in organizing and outlining a speech is to create the ______ points.

49. Speaking professionals recommend that the actual speaking outline be prepared using the ______ format.

50. In the ______ outline, each section of the speech (introduction, body, and conclusion) should be labeled.

51. A(n) ______ outline is the briefest form of outline.

52. A(n) ______ outline uses partial construction of the sentence form of each point.

53. A type of outline not recommended in the delivery of most speeches is the ______ outline.

54. ______ outlines are often the preferred speaking outline format.

55. Speeches that are carefully planned and practiced in advance and then delivered from a key-word or phrase outline are known as ______ speeches.

56. The ______ outline restricts eye contact with the audience.

57. The speaking outline should be prepared on ______.

58. A(n) ______ outline should contain just enough words to jog a speaker's memory.

59. The key to the successful delivery of a speech is ______.

ESSAY AND SHORT ANSWER QUESTIONS

60. How can a speaker prepare a speech by using a working outline?

61. Why should a working outline be prepared in a full-sentence format?

62. Identify the steps involved in creating a working outline.

63. Explain the difference between a phrase outline and a key-word outline.

64. List one advantage and one disadvantage of a sentence outline.

65. Name the outline format that is the easiest for a prepared speaker to follow, and explain why.

66. Explain why it is important to condense the working outline into a key-word outline.

67. In a speaking outline, how should a speaker indicate transitions, sources to cite, and presentation aids to be used in the speech?

68. Identify the steps involved in creating a speaking outline.

ANSWER KEY FOR CHAPTER 13

1. True (p. 192)
2. True (p. 193)
3. True (p. 192)
4. True (p. 192)
5. False (p. 192)
6. True (p. 192)
7. False (p. 192)
8. True (p. 192)
9. True (p. 192)
10. False (p. 193)
11. True (p. 193)
12. False (p. 193)
13. True (p. 193)
14. False (p. 193)
15. True (p. 195)
16. True (p. 196)
17. False (p. 194)
18. True (p. 194)
19. True (p. 194)
20. False (p. 194)
21. True (p. 194)
22. False (p. 194)
23. True (p. 194)
24. True (p. 194)
25. False (p. 201)
26. False (p. 195)
27. True (p. 195)
28. True (p. 200)
29. True (p. 202)
30. A (p. 192)
31. A (p. 193)
32. D (p. 194)
33. C (p. 194)
34. D (p. 194)
35. C (p. 194)
36. D (pp. 200–201)
37. B (p. 196)
38. working; speaking or delivery (p. 192)
39. outlines (p. 192)
40. working (p. 192)
41. working (p. 192)
42. speaking or delivery (p. 192)
43. phrases (p. 192)
44. sentence (p. 192)
45. Key-word (p. 194)
46. sentence (p. 194)
47. sentence (p. 193)
48. main (p. 196)
49. key-word (p. 193)
50. working (p. 196)
51. key-word (p. 194)
52. phrase (p. 194)
53. sentence (p. 194)
54. Key-word (p. 194)
55. extemporaneous (p. 194)
56. full-sentence (p. 194)
57. notecards or small sheets of paper (p. 201)
58. speaking (p. 200)
59. practice (p. 202)
60. (No answer, p. 192)
61. (No answer, pp. 192–193)
62. (No answer, p. 193)
63. (No answer, p. 194)
64. (No answer, pp. 193–194)
65. (No answer, p. 194)
66. (No answer, p. 194)
67. (No answer, p. 195)
68. (No answer, p. 202)

14 *Developing the Introduction*

TRUE/FALSE QUESTIONS

1. If the body of the speech is well-developed, it is sometimes an effective technique to deliver the introduction and conclusion spontaneously, without preparation.
2. The introduction and the conclusion of the speech are more important than the body.
3. An effective conclusion can help the audience remember a speech.
4. The choices a speaker makes about the introduction of a speech do not affect the outcome of the entire speech.
5. Audience members decide in the first five seconds of a speech whether they will give their full attention to the speaker and believe what he or she has to say.
6. Supporting material should not be used to open a speech.
7. The first challenge a speaker faces in developing an introduction is to win the audience's attention.
8. In an introduction, using a quotation from someone who is not famous will discredit the speaker.
9. Using a story in an introduction can make the speaker's ideas concrete and colorful.
10. After using a real or hypothetical story to introduce a speech, the speaker should be sure to explain exactly what the story means.
11. A rhetorical question posed by the speaker seeks a direct response from the audience.
12. Polling audience members during the speech introduction is an effective way to gain their attention.
13. A speaker who poses a question that seeks an actual response from the audience risks encountering unexpected responses.
14. Speakers who introduce their speeches with startling statements or unusual information are ineffective in gaining the audience's attention.

15. Introducing a speech with a short joke or a funny story sets a positive tone for what is to follow.

16. When using humor in an introduction, the speaker should keep in mind that the humor should relate to the speech topic and occasion.

17. Audiences are unaffected by whether or not a speaker shows that they share similar interests and goals.

18. Self-deprecating humor in a speech introduction is always inappropriate.

19. Humor breakdowns can occur when audience members do not share the same cultural assumptions as the speaker.

20. Introductions that include references to the speech occasion and the audience tend to capture audience attention and establish goodwill.

21. Focusing on the audience in the introduction demonstrates interest and respect.

22. Speech humor should match the audience, topic, purpose, and occasion..

23. The speech introduction should capture the audience's attention, but it does not need to delve into the topic and purpose of the speech.

24. When speakers use the technique of previewing in an introduction, they state the main points of the speech.

25. Introductory previews should be long and complicated.

26. Previewing helps the audience mentally organize a speech.

27. A speech introduction should identify the speech topic and purpose.

28. Audience members are usually motivated to listen to a message that they think is relevant to them.

29. Explaining to audience members what they have to gain by listening to you is not effective in motivating an audience to accept the goals of your speech.

30. To build credibility in the introduction, a speaker should make a simple statement of his or her qualifications for speaking on the topic.

31. The introduction should be prepared first, as it is the first part of the speech.

32. As a rule, the length of the introduction should be no more than 20 to 25 percent of the speech body.

MULTIPLE-CHOICE QUESTIONS

33. A speech introduction is designed to
    A) arouse the audience's attention and motivate the audience to accept the speaker's goals.
    B) provide an in-depth discussion of the topic.
    C) review and discuss all the main points of a speech.
    D) do all of the above.

34. Which of the following can be used to effectively introduce or conclude a speech?
    A) examples
    B) stories
    C) questions
    D) all of the above

35. The first challenge faced by the speaker in the introduction of the speech is to win the audience's
    A) attention.
    B) approval.
    C) admiration.
    D) acceptance.

36. In her speech about friendship, Becky opened her speech by stating, "As Vanessa Smith has written, 'Many people will walk in and out of your life, but only true friends will leave footprints in your heart.'" Becky began her introduction by using
    A) repetition.
    B) a startling statement.
    C) a quotation.
    D) imagery.

37. Using a story as a speech introduction
    A) personalizes issues.
    B) makes ideas irrelevant.
    C) discourages identification.
    D) does none of the above.

38. Which of the following is a potential drawback to polling audience members during the introduction?
    A) No one will respond.
    B) Responses will be unexpected.
    C) The speaker may be put on the spot to answer.
    D) All of the above.

39. Speakers frequently base their startling statements on
    A) statistics.
    B) humor.
    C) attitudes.
    D) all of the above.

40. Speech humor should always match
    A) the audience.
    B) the topic.
    C) the occasion.
    D) all of the above.

41. An effective introduction should
    A) capture your audience's attention.
    B) comprise at least 25 percent of your total speech.

C) be prepared before the body of the speech.
D) all of the above.

42. Previewing the speech in the introduction
A) tells the audience the order in which the main points will be addressed.
B) addresses the tone rather than the organization of the speech.
C) often "gives away" the entire content of the speech.
D) does all of the above.

43. A good introduction demonstrates why the audience should care above all about a speaker's
A) opinions.
B) topic.
C) purpose.
D) supporting material.

44. During the speech introduction, the audience decides whether or not they are interested in the topic and the speaker. To build credibility, a speaker should establish his or her
A) family background.
B) supporting material.
C) qualifications.
D) logos.

45. Generally, the introduction should be brief and no more than ______ percent of the speech body.
A) 5 to 10
B) 10 to 15
C) 15 to 20
D) 20 to 25

FILL-IN-THE-BLANK QUESTIONS

46. The speaker's first step in the speech introduction is to gain the audience's ________.

47. Used to introduce a speech, a(n) ______ can be from literature, poetry, film, or people.

48. Language expert William Safire once remarked that ______ are "surefire attention getters."

49. Questions that do not invite audience responses are called ______ questions.

50. Speakers frequently base their introductory startling statements on ______.

51. When using ______ in an introduction, the speaker should keep in mind that it should relate to the speech topic and occasion and should not belittle others.

52. Humor breakdowns can occur when audience members do not share the same ______ assumptions as the speaker.

53. The technique of ______ the main points helps the audience mentally organize the speech and helps the speaker maintain the audience's attention.

54. Describing a speech topic's practical implications to the audience helps make the topic ______ to the audience.

55. When a speaker states his or her qualifications in the speech introduction, this helps build speaker ______.

56. The speech introduction should be prepared ______ the speaker has completed the speech body.

ESSAY AND SHORT ANSWER QUESTIONS

57. Explain how the speech introduction prepares an audience to listen to a speech.

58. Why is it important for a speaker to prepare the introduction and conclusion just as thoroughly as the speech body?

59. List three functions of a good introduction.

60. Give an example of a quotation to introduce a speech.

61. Write a brief introduction that begins with the following quotation by Maya Angelou: "When people show you who they are, believe them."

62. Give an example of a rhetorical question to introduce a speech.

63. Name two hazards that may occur when a speaker asks a question that seeks an actual response from the audience.

64. Name two general guidelines for using a story in a speech.

65. List three rules that a speaker should keep in mind when using humor in a speech.

66. During the introduction, how can a speaker express a genuine interest in the audience?

67. Give an example of previewing in an introduction.

68. Why is it so important for a speaker to use the introduction to establish the relevance of the topic to the audience?

69. Explain why the introduction should be written after the speech body.

70. List three guidelines for preparing an introduction.

ANSWER KEY FOR CHAPTER 14

1. False (p. 215)
2. False (p. 215)
3. True (p. 215)
4. False (p. 215)
5. False (p. 215)
6. False (p. 215)
7. True (p. 215)
8. False (p. 216)
9. True (p. 216)
10. False (p. 217)
11. False (p. 217)
12. True (p. 217)
13. True (p. 217)
14. False (p. 218)
15. True (p. 218)
16. True (p. 218)
17. False (p. 219)
18. False (p. 219)
19. True (p. 220)
20. True (p. 219)
21. True (p. 219)
22. True (p. 218)
23. False (p. 219)
24. True (p. 220)
25. False (p. 220)
26. True (p. 220)
27. True (p. 220)
28. True (p. 221)
29. False (p. 221)
30. True (p. 222)
31. False (p. 222)
32. False (p. 222)
33. A (p. 215)
34. D (p. 215)
35. A (p. 215)
36. C (p. 216)
37. A (p. 216)
38. D (p. 217)
39. A (p. 218)
40. D (p. 218)
41. A (p. 215)
42. A (p. 220)
43. B (p. 221)
44. C (p. 222)
45. B (p. 222)
46. attention (p. 215)
47. quotation (p. 215)
48. stories (p. 216)
49. rhetorical (p. 217)
50. statistics (p. 218)
51. humor (p. 218)
52. cultural (p. 220)
53. previewing (p. 220)
54. relevant (p. 221)
55. credibility (p. 222)
56. after (p. 222)
57. (No answer, p. 215)
58. (No answer, p. 215)
59. (No answer, p. 215)
60. (No answer, p. 216)
61. (No answer)
62. (No answer, p. 217)
63. (No answer, p. 217)
64. (No answer, p. 216)
65. (No answer, p. 218)
66. (No answer, p. 219)
67. (No answer, p. 220)
68. (No answer, pp. 221–222)
69. (No answer, p. 222)
70. (No answer, p. 222)

15 *Developing the Conclusion*

TRUE/FALSE QUESTIONS

1. A conclusion signals the end of the speech and provides closure.
2. A transition statement or phrase is one way to alert the audience that a speech is coming to an end.
3. As a general rule, the conclusion should comprise about one-third of the speech.
4. A speaker can effectively signal closure by adjusting the manner of delivery.
5. A conclusion gives the speaker the opportunity to drive home his or her purpose and a final chance to reinforce the main points of the speech.
6. In the conclusion, the speaker should not reiterate the topic and speech purpose.
7. A strong conclusion challenges audience members to put to use what the speaker has taught them.
8. In informative speeches, the concluding challenge comes in the form of a call to action.
9. Quotations, stories, and questions are appropriate ways to conclude a speech.
10. Using a quotation that captures the essence of the speech can be a very effective way to close a speech.
11. A concluding story can bring the entire speech into focus and can help the audience visualize the speech.
12. Rhetorical questions are not effective conclusions.
13. Like the introduction, the conclusion of a speech should be prepared before the speech body.
14. A speaker should carefully consider the use of language in the conclusion.

MULTIPLE-CHOICE QUESTIONS

15. Conclusions provide
    A) the speaker the opportunity to drive home the speech purpose.
    B) the speaker a final chance to make an impression that accomplishes the speech goals.
    C) the audience with a sense of logical and emotional closure.
    D) all of the above.

16. An effective conclusion should always
    A) include an effective quote.
    B) make the speech memorable.
    C) introduce the last main point.
    D) do all of the above.

17. The conclusion should comprise about ______ of the speech.
    A) one-half
    B) one-third
    C) one-sixth
    D) one-eighth

18. Speech conclusions fulfill which of the following functions?
    A) alerting the audience that the speech is coming to an end
    B) summarizing the key points of the speech
    C) challenging the audience to respond
    D) all of the above

19. The summary portion of the speech conclusion should *not*
    A) "tell the audience what you've already told them."
    B) mention each main point of the speech.
    C) mention each supporting point of the speech.
    D) comment on the significance of each main point.

20. Effective speech conclusions often employ
    A) many of the same techniques used in introductions.
    B) techniques that are not used in introductions.
    C) expert opinions and advice.
    D) all of the above.

21. When the speaker reiterates each main point in the conclusion, the audience
    A) mentally checks off what they have heard during the speech.
    B) secretly hopes that the speech will hurry up and end.
    C) asks the speaker to review the supporting points.
    D) all of the above.

22. A concluding challenge by a speaker that asks an audience to act in response to the speech is termed a
    A) persuasive attempt.
    B) call to action.
    C) reiteration.
    D) signpost.

23. Listeners are most likely to remember and act on a speech that
    A) uses many statistics.
    B) ends with a strong conclusion.
    C) begins with a quotation.
    D) does all of the above.

FILL-IN-THE-BLANK QUESTIONS

24. The ______ provides the speaker a final opportunity to leave the desired impression on the audience.

25. Using a(n) ______ statement or phrase, such as *finally* or *looking back,* is one way to alert the audience that a speech is coming to an end.

26. A call to ______ is a speaker's concluding challenge to the audience to act in response to the speech.

27. Quotations, stories, and questions are appropriate ways to ______ a speech.

28. Like the introduction, the conclusion of a speech should be prepared ______ the speech body.

ESSAY AND SHORT ANSWER QUESTIONS

29. List three functions of a conclusion.

30. How can a conclusion effectively summarize the main points and goals of a speech?

31. Explain how a challenge issued during a conclusion varies for an informative and a persuasive speech.

32. Discuss three ways that a speaker can make a conclusion memorable.

33. What are three things a speaker can assess to determine whether the conclusion is effective?

34. Give an example of a concluding rhetorical question.

35. Name three guidelines for preparing a conclusion.

36. Give two tips for practicing the delivery of a speech conclusion.

ANSWER KEY FOR CHAPTER 15

1. True (p. 223)
2. True (p. 223)
3. False (p. 223)
4. True (p. 223)
5. True (p. 223)
6. False (p. 224)
7. True (p. 224)
8. False (p. 224)
9. True (p. 226)
10. True (p. 226)
11. True (p. 227)
12. False (p. 227)
13. False (p. 227)
14. True (p. 227)
15. D (p. 223)
16. B (p. 225)
17. C (p. 227)
18. D (p. 223)
19. C (p. 224)
20. A (p. 226)
21. A (p. 224)
22. B (p. 224)
23. B (p. 224)
24. conclusion (p. 223)
25. transitional (p. 223)
26. action (p. 224)
27. conclude (p. 226)
28. after (p. 227)
29. (No answer, p. 223)
30. (No answer, p. 224)
31. (No answer, p. 224)
32. (No answer, pp. 225–227)
33. (No answer, p. 226)
34. (No answer, p. 227)
35. (No answer, pp. 227–228)
36. (No answer, p. 227)

16 *Using Language to Style the Speech*

TRUE/FALSE QUESTIONS

1. Rhetorical devices are techniques of language that speakers use to express their ideas in order to achieve their speech purpose.

2. Oral language is generally more interactive with the audience than is written language.

3. Speeches make less frequent use of repetition and transitions than do most forms of written communication.

4. Through language, humans define and create culture.

5. Since few contemporary audiences are culturally diverse, a speaker need not be aware of or sensitive to cultural variations in language.

6. Cultural sensitivity is a purely unconscious, instinctive way of judging cultural beliefs, norms, or traditions that are different from your own.

7. Language that relies on unfounded assumptions, negative descriptions, or stereotypes of a given group's characteristics is termed *biased language.*

8. Audiences are generally not offended when the speaker repeatedly uses the generic pronoun *he.*

9. The specialized language of a given profession is called *filibustering.*

10. Listeners prefer complex language over simple language in a speech.

11. Abstract language is specific, tangible, and definite.

12. Concise spoken language includes the use of contractions, phrases, and sentence fragments.

13. The words *old, thing, big,* and *bad* are examples of abstract language.

14. A speaker who describes activities and objects with colorful and concrete language helps create a vivid image for the audience or appeals to their senses.

15. A metaphor compares one thing to another, using *like* or *as* to do so.

16. An analogy compares an unfamiliar concept to a more familiar one in order to increase audience understanding of the unfamiliar concept.

17. *Love is a rose* is an example of a simile.

18. *Irony* refers to endowing abstract ideas or inanimate objects with human qualities.

19. A speaker's use or misuse of language has a significant effect on the level of credibility he or she establishes with the audience.

20. Figures of speech include similes, metaphors, and analogies.

21. The connotative meaning is the literal, or dictionary, definition of a word.

22. In the sentence *Tom invited Maria on a date,* the active voice is used.

23. Repetition is an effective strategy for using language in a speech.

24. Alliteration is the arrangement of words, phrases, or sentences in a similar form.

25. Parallelism is the repetition of the same sounds, usually initial consonants, in two or more neighboring words or syllables.

MULTIPLE-CHOICE QUESTIONS

26. Types of vivid imagery include
    A) repetition.
    B) hyperbole.
    C) transitions.
    D) internal previews.

27. Which of the following represents a difference between spoken and written language?
    A) Spoken language is often more interactive with the audience.
    B) Writers use more personal pronouns than speakers do.
    C) Speakers use more obscure terms than writers do.
    D) both A and B

28. A culturally sensitive speaker
    A) avoids language that is biased.
    B) makes a conscious effort to be considerate of cultural differences.
    C) adapts language to a diverse audience.
    D) does all of the above.

29. The term *biased language* refers to language that is
    A) ageist or homophobic.
    B) sexist or racist.
    C) both A and B.
    D) neither A nor B.

30. An example of a pronoun that is commonly overused in a sexist manner is
    A) *it.*
    B) *they.*
    C) *he.*
    D) *our.*

31. A speaker's use of sexist pronouns
    A) unnecessarily restricts the gender of the person(s) the speaker is referring to.
    B) offends only females.
    C) makes a speaker appear credible but not intelligent.
    D) aids audience understanding.

32. How many people in the United States experience a mental or physical disability?
    A) one in three
    B) one in five
    C) one in eight
    D) one in ten

33. A speaker who uses vivid imagery
    A) diminishes meaning.
    B) distracts listeners from the main point of the speech.
    C) invites listeners to use their imaginations.
    D) does none of the above.

34. In Leeza's presentation on her graduate school experiences, she said, "Graduate school is an uphill battle." Leeza used which figure of speech?
    A) simile
    B) metaphor
    C) analogy
    D) alliteration

35. Forms of expression that create striking comparisons to help listeners visualize, identify with, and understand the speaker's ideas are called
    A) alliteration.
    B) libelous language.
    C) figures of speech.
    D) conjunctions.

36. A speaker should avoid using expressions that are
    A) clichés.
    B) analogies.
    C) appealing to the senses.
    D) all of the above.

37. *His character plays a rocking, rolling, roaring, raging role.* This statement best illustrates which of the following techniques?
    A) simile
    B) metaphor
    C) personification
    D) alliteration

38. *His lies are a house of cards.* This statement best illustrates which of the following techniques?
    A) simile
    B) metaphor
    C) personification
    D) alliteration

39. Effective speakers are careful to use language that is appropriate to
    A) the audience.
    B) the occasion.
    C) the subject matter.
    D) all of the above.

40. The literal, dictionary definition of a word is its
    A) hyperbolic meaning.
    B) analogous meaning.
    C) denotative meaning.
    D) connotative meaning.

41. When people disagree about the meaning of a word, they are responding to the word's
    A) denotative meaning.
    B) connotative meaning.
    C) libelous meaning.
    D) abstract meaning.

42. One way that a speaker can leave a lasting impression on listeners is to incorporate oral language that is artfully arranged and infused with rhythm. One device that helps a speaker accomplish this specific purpose is
    A) repetition.
    B) personification.
    C) analogy.
    D) none of the above.

43. Parallelism can be used by a speaker
    A) to create a powerful and poetic effect for the audience.
    B) to orally enumerate the speech's main points.
    C) in the form of pairs or triads.
    D) in all of the above ways.

FILL-IN-THE-BLANK QUESTIONS

44. ______ language is generally more interactive and inclusive of the audience than is written language.

45. Speeches make more frequent use of repetition and transitions than do most forms of ______ communication.

46. Through language, humans define and create ______.

47. ______ expressions are regional variations on expressions, and may confuse listeners.

48. Cultural ______ is a conscious attempt to be considerate of cultural beliefs, norms, or traditions different from your own.

49. Language that relies on unfounded assumptions, negative descriptions, or stereotypes of a given group's characteristics is termed ______ language.

50. When a speaker repeatedly uses the generic pronoun *he* to refer to both men and women, the speaker is using ______ language.

51. The specialized language of a given profession is called ______.

52. ______ language is specific, tangible, and definite.

53. A(n) ______ explicitly compares one thing to another, using *like* or *as* to do so.

54. A(n) ______ compares an unfamiliar concept to a more familiar one in order to increase audience understanding of the unfamiliar concept.

55. ______ refers to endowing abstract ideas or inanimate objects with human qualities.

56. The ______ meaning of a word is its literal, or dictionary, definition.

57. The ______ meaning of a word is the special association that different people bring to bear on it.

58. ______ is the repetition of the same sounds, usually initial consonants, in two or more neighboring words or syllables.

ESSAY AND SHORT ANSWER QUESTIONS

59. List three ways in which spoken and written language differ.

60. Why is it important for a speaker to display cultural sensitivity through the use of unbiased language?

61. Why does a speaker's use of jargon often exasperate an audience?

62. Explain why speakers should strive for simplicity in language.

63. Why are speeches that contain mostly concrete words and phrases more effective than speeches that rely solely on abstract language?

64. How can a speaker create vivid imagery for the audience?

65. Explain the difference between a metaphor and a simile.

66. Define *personification* and give an example.

67. Define *hyperbole* and give an example.

68. Why is it important for a speaker to understand the connotative meanings of words?

69. Explain and give an example of a rhetorical device that a speaker can use to create effective rhythm and a lasting impression in his or her speech.

ANSWER KEY FOR CHAPTER 16

1. True (p. 229)
2. True (p. 230)
3. False (p. 230)
4. True (p. 234)
5. False (p. 234)
6. False (p. 234)
7. True (p. 234)
8. False (p. 234)
9. False (p. 230)
10. False (p. 230)
11. False (p. 235)
12. True (pp. 230, 232)
13. True (p. 236)
14. True (p. 237)
15. False (p. 237)
16. True (p. 237)
17. False (p. 237)
18. False (p. 238)
19. True (p. 239)
20. True (p. 237)
21. False (p. 239)
22. True (p. 240)
23. True (p. 241)
24. False (p. 242)
25. False (p. 243)
26. B (p. 238)
27. A (p. 230)
28. D (p. 234)
29. C (p. 234)
30. C (p. 234)
31. A (p. 234)
32. B (p. 234)
33. C (p. 237)
34. B (p. 237)
35. C (p. 237)
36. A (p. 237)
37. D (p. 242)
38. B (p. 237)
39. D (p. 239)
40. C (p. 239)
41. B (p. 239)
42. A (p. 241)
43. D (p. 243)
44. Oral or spoken (p. 230)
45. written (p. 234)
46. culture (p. 234)
47. Colloquial (p. 234)
48. sensitivity (p. 234)
49. biased (p. 234)
50. sexist (p. 234)
51. jargon (p. 230)
52. Concrete (p. 235)
53. simile (p. 237)
54. analogy (p. 237)
55. Personification (p. 238)
56. denotative (p. 239)
57. connotative (p. 239)
58. Alliteration (p. 242)
59. (No answer, pp. 229–230)
60. (No answer, pp. 234–235)
61. (No answer, p. 230)
62. (No answer, p. 230)
63. (No answer, pp. 235–236)
64. (No answer, pp. 237–238)
65. (No answer, p. 237)
66. (No answer, p. 238)
67. (No answer, p. 238)
68. (No answer, p. 239)
69. (No answer, pp. 241–243)

17 *Methods of Delivery*

TRUE/FALSE QUESTIONS

1. It is important for a speaker to incorporate elements of conversational style in delivering a speech.
2. Effective delivery is quite different from everyday conversation in that it relies on complex, stylized gestures.
3. Delivery is a critical part of successful speechmaking.
4. Speakers who lack enthusiasm often lose their audience's attention.
5. A speaker's lack of confidence is rarely apparent to his or her audience.
6. A speaker can build rapport with his or her audience by making the message relevant to the audience and by using direct delivery.
7. Speaking from a manuscript is most useful when the speaker is required to be very precise in his or her message.
8. Speaking from memory is the most natural way to deliver a message.
9. Speaking from a manuscript is considered best for brief speeches, such as toasts and introductions.
10. Delivering a speech without prior preparation is called *speaking extemporaneously.*
11. Most public speeches are delivered extemporaneously.
12. Impromptu delivery is the most widely used form of delivery in public speaking.
13. Delivery can be used for both ethical and unethical purposes.
14. A speaker should always reveal the speech purpose to the audience.

MULTIPLE-CHOICE QUESTIONS

15. Effective speech delivery should be all of the following:
    A) natural, monotone, confident, and comfortable.
    B) natural, self-deprecating, direct, and abstract.
    C) natural, enthusiastic, confident, and direct.
    D) natural, confident, extremely formal, and animated.

16. A speaker can feel confident that his or her delivery has a relaxed, natural quality if
    A) the message is presented with cheerfulness.
    B) the speaker's behavior does not call undue attention to itself.
    C) the speaker focuses more on self and less on audience.
    D) all of the above are accomplished.

17. A speaker can establish a direct connection with listeners by
    A) maintaining eye contact.
    B) using animated facial expressions.
    C) using a friendly tone of voice.
    D) doing all of the above.

18. Speaking from a manuscript
    A) is useful when precise messages are required.
    B) encourages eye contact.
    C) encourages naturalness.
    D) is best in informal settings.

19. Speaking from memory
    A) is a natural way to present a message.
    B) stifles authentic and sincere enthusiasm.
    C) is the most popular delivery method.
    D) should not be used for toasts or introductions.

20. The formal name for speaking from memory is
    A) oratory.
    B) manuscript.
    C) impromptu.
    D) extemporaneous.

21. Which type of delivery worries speakers because they have little time to gather their thoughts and achieve composure?
    A) memorized
    B) manuscript
    C) impromptu
    D) extemporaneous

22. The word *impromptu* means
    A) improvised and unpracticed.
    B) provocative and spontaneous.
    C) lively and personal.
    D) none of the above.

23. Which type of delivery falls somewhere between impromptu and memorized?
    A) unpracticed
    B) manuscript
    C) extemporaneous
    D) all of the above

24. The method of speech delivery that is most flexible for the speaker and preferred by listeners is
    A) extemporaneous speaking.
    B) speaking from memory.
    C) impromptu speaking.
    D) speaking from manuscript.

FILL-IN-THE-BLANK QUESTIONS

25. In a speech, the skillful application of natural conversational behavior is termed effective ______.

26. Effective delivery has many elements in common with everyday ______.

27. Speaking from ______ is most useful when the speaker is required to be very precise in his or her message.

28. The delivery method known as ______ speaking is the most natural way to deliver a speech.

29. Speaking from ______ requires the speaker to recall exact words, which may result in the speaker's having a mental block at some point.

30. When a speaker delivers a speech without any prior preparation, he or she is giving a(n) ______ delivery.

31. Speaking from ______ is an appropriate type of delivery for brief speeches, such as toasts and introductions.

32. Most public speeches are given using ______ delivery.

33. Speaking ______ is the term for giving a prepared and practiced speech without memorizing it or reading it word for word from a text.

34. Trustworthiness, responsibility, respect, and fairness are the qualities that characterize ______ delivery.

ESSAY AND SHORT ANSWER QUESTIONS

35. Explain why speech delivery should strive for natural, rather than theatrical, behavior.

36. How can a speaker project a sense of confidence and competence?

37. What happens when speakers focus on themselves rather than on the message?

38. List three ways for a speaker to establish a direct connection with an audience when delivering a speech.

39. Identify two ways in which speakers can make a delivery seem more natural when they are reading from a prepared text.

40. Why should a speaker avoid memorizing an entire speech?

41. List two tips for impromptu speaking.

42. Compare and contrast these two methods of speech delivery: speaking impromptu and speaking extemporaneously.

43. As an audience member, which of the four methods of speech delivery do you prefer? Give three reasons why you prefer this particular method.

ANSWER KEY FOR CHAPTER 17

1. True (p. 252)
2. False (p. 252)
3. True (p. 252)
4. True (p. 253)
5. False (p. 253)
6. True (p. 253)
7. True (p. 254)
8. False (p. 255)
9. False (p. 256)
10. False (p. 257)
11. True (p. 257)
12. False (p. 257)
13. True (p. 258)
14. True (p. 258)
15. C (p. 252)
16. B (p. 252)
17. D (p. 253)
18. A (p. 254)
19. B (pp. 255–256)
20. A (p. 255)
21. C (p. 257)
22. A (p. 256)
23. C (p. 257)
24. A (p. 258)
25. delivery (p. 252)
26. conversation (p. 252)
27. manuscript (p. 254)
28. extemporaneous (p. 254)
29. memory (p. 256)
30. impromptu (p. 254)
31. memory (p. 254)
32. extemporaneous (p. 257)
33. extemporaneously (p. 257)
34. ethical (p. 258)
35. (No answer, p. 252)
36. (No answer, p. 253)
37. (No answer, p. 253)
38. (No answer, p. 253)
39. (No answer, p. 254)
40. (No answer, pp. 255–256)
41. (No answer, pp. 256–257)
42. (No answer, pp. 256–258)
43. (No answer)

The Voice in Delivery 18

TRUE/FALSE QUESTIONS

1. Pitch is the relative loudness of a speaker's voice while giving a speech.
2. The proper volume for delivering a speech is somewhat louder than that of normal conversation.
3. When adjusting speaking volume, a speaker should consider the size of the room and the number of people in the audience.
4. The speaker's mouth should be positioned one to three inches from the microphone.
5. Pitch represents the range of sounds from high to low.
6. When there is no variety in pitch, speaking becomes monotonous.
7. Public speakers should strive to vary the rate of speaking.
8. Novice speakers usually pause for too long a time at dramatic moments in a speech.
9. Unnecessary and undesirable words used to fill pauses are called *vocal fillers.*
10. Volume, pitch, rate, and pauses work independently of each other.
11. Delivering a speech with the vocal variety that English speakers in the United States expect can be very challenging for non-native speakers.
12. Enthusiasm is one key to achieving vocal variety in a speech.
13. A speaker's overexcitement may result in a consistently low pitch.
14. Pronunciation is the clarity or forcefulness in saying words so they are audible and discernible.
15. Incorrect pronunciations are often a matter of habit.
16. A speaker's cultural dialect may be distracting to the audience.
17. Articulation problems are much rarer than pronunciation problems and are usually very difficult to overcome.

18. If a speaker tends to mumble, he or she should practice speaking louder and with emphatic pronunciation.

MULTIPLE-CHOICE QUESTIONS

19. The proper volume for delivering a speech depends on which of the following factors?
    A) the size of the room and number of persons in the audience
    B) the availability of a microphone
    C) background noise
    D) all of the above

20. Speakers whose volume is too ______ are viewed less positively than those who project their voices at a pleasing volume.
    A) low
    B) enthusiastic
    C) monotone
    D) fast

21. Pitch is
    A) the relative loudness of a speaker's voice.
    B) the speed at which a speaker talks.
    C) the rate at which a speaker stops and starts.
    D) the range of sounds a speaker's voice produces from high to low.

22. What term refers to the rising and falling of voice pitch across phrases and sentences, which can result in the same word or phrase conveying two different meanings? (For example: "It's time to study already." "It's time to study alREADY?")
    A) rate
    B) intonation
    C) volume
    D) articulation

23. After Bill practiced his speech in front of his friends, they informed him that he often said "um" and "er." To change this distracting pattern, Bill set a goal for himself to replace his vocal fillers with
    A) the phrase *as you may know.*
    B) extended pauses.
    C) slight pauses.
    D) all of the above.

24. One key to achieving effective vocal variety is
    A) enthusiasm.
    B) visual aids.
    C) pronunciation.
    D) monotony.

25. Incorrect word pronunciations
    A) are a matter of habit.
    B) distract the audience.
    C) cannot be improved by clear articulation.
    D) all of the above.

FILL-IN-THE-BLANK QUESTIONS

26. ______ is the relative loudness of a speaker's voice while giving a speech.

27. The proper volume for delivering a speech is somewhat ______ than that of normal conversation.

28. A speaker should adjust the speaking ______ to the size of the room and the number of people in the audience.

29. The speaker's mouth should be positioned about ______ inches from a handheld or fixed microphone.

30. The range of sounds from high to low is known as ______.

31. Novice speakers are especially uncomfortable with ______.

32. Unnecessary and undesirable words used to fill pauses are called ______.

33. Enthusiasm is one key to achieving ______ variety.

34. Cultural or regional variations in pronunciation and articulation are known as ______.

ESSAY AND SHORT ANSWER QUESTIONS

35. Explain how a speaker can learn to adjust his or her speaking volume.

36. Identify three tips for using a microphone when delivering a speech.

37. List two ways a speaker can avoid a monotonous speaking style.

38. Give an example of vocal fillers, and explain why they distract from the speech message.

39. What are two things a speaker can do to correct articulation and pronunciation problems?

40. Explain the difference between pronunciation and articulation. Why are these elements of a speaker's vocal delivery so important?

ANSWER KEY FOR CHAPTER 18

1. False (p. 260)
2. True (p. 260)
3. True (p. 260)
4. False (p. 261)
5. True (p. 261)
6. True (p. 261)
7. True (p. 262)
8. False (p. 262)
9. True (p. 262)
10. False (p. 263)
11. True (p. 263)
12. True (p. 264)
13. False (p. 262)
14. False (p. 264)
15. True (p. 265)
16. True (p. 264)
17. False (p. 265)
18. True (p. 265)
19. D (p. 260)
20. A (p. 260)
21. D (p. 261)
22. B (p. 261)
23. C (p. 262)
24. A (p. 264)
25. D (p. 265)
26. Volume (p. 260)
27. louder (p. 260)
28. volume (p. 260)
29. six (p. 261)
30. pitch (p. 261)
31. pauses (p. 262)
32. vocal fillers (p. 262)
33. vocal (p. 264)
34. dialects (p. 264)
35. (No answer, p. 260)
36. (No answer, p. 261)
37. (No answer, pp. 261–262)
38. (No answer, p. 262)
39. (No answer, p. 265)
40. (No answer, pp. 264–265)

The Body in Delivery 19

TRUE/FALSE QUESTIONS

1. In addition to spoken words, audiences receive information from a speech through aural and visual channels.

2. *Paralanguage* refers to *what* is said, not *how* something is said.

3. According to one study, listeners may derive only 7 percent of a message's meaning from the words a speaker uses.

4. Nonverbal communication clarifies the meaning of verbal messages.

5. Nonverbal communication does not help to establish speaker credibility.

6. Listeners use various bodily cues to communicate their pleasure or displeasure with a speech.

7. Coughing and excessive shifting around by the audience may indicate difficulty in hearing and flagging interest in a speech.

8. Nonverbal behavior allows the speaker to adjust his or her relationship with an audience.

9. Moving out from behind a podium and walking or standing among audience members establishes a formal speech atmosphere.

10. Nonverbal communication plays a key part in the audience's perception of the speaker's credibility.

11. Audience members respond less positively to speakers whom they perceive to be well dressed because such speakers are intimidating.

12. Audience members usually cannot detect discrepancies between what the speaker says and how he or she says it.

13. Smiling is an effective way for a speaker to build rapport with an audience.

14. A speaker's deadpan facial expression encourages an audience's attention.

15. Hand gestures are the most important nonverbal behavior in public speaking.

16. Scanning is a technique whereby speakers briefly gaze at all members of the audience.

17. A speaker's gestures should arise from genuine emotions and should conform to the speaker's personality.

18. If space and time allow, a speaker should try to get out from behind the podium and stand with the audience.

19. How a speaker dresses when delivering a speech is unimportant.

20. Gestures have different meanings in different cultures.

21. Gesturing with a pen is one of the more effective nonverbal delivery techniques.

22. Practicing your speech by actually going through the motions is not vital to effective delivery.

23. A speaker who focuses on the message makes the speech delivery more natural and confident.

24. Practicing a speech in front of someone and gaining constructive criticism is helpful for speakers.

25. Speakers should avoid tape-recording or videotaping rehearsals of the speech.

26. After rehearsing aloud, a speaker will often revise the speaking outline.

27. When rehearsing a speech, the speaker should try to simulate the actual speech setting but should not practice in front of people.

28. When rehearsing a speech, it is not important for the speaker to time the speech.

29. The introduction and conclusion should make up no more than 10 to 15 percent of the entire speech.

30. Speaking experts recommend practicing a speech at least five times in its final form.

MULTIPLE-CHOICE QUESTIONS

31. The aural channel, or a speaker's use of paralanguage, includes
    A) volume and pitch.
    B) rate and pauses.
    C) vocal variety, articulation, and pronunciation.
    D) all of the above.

32. Nonverbal communication
    A) diminishes the meaning of verbal messages.
    B) complicates feedback.
    C) helps establish speaker credibility and a relationship with the audience.
    D) increases the ultimate pitch of a speech.

33. When a speaker is alert to the audience's ______, he or she can respond to it and make the audience feel respected and recognized.
    A) feedback
    B) credibility
    C) vocal variety
    D) articulation

34. Audiences are more readily persuaded by speakers who emphasize
    A) eye contact.
    B) nodding at listeners.
    C) vocal variety.
    D) all of the above.

35. Which talk show host pioneered a sense of informality with the audience?
    A) Oprah Winfrey
    B) David Letterman
    C) Phil Donahue
    D) Conan O'Brien

36. If an audience member perceives a speaker as unattractive, the audience member is apt to
    A) respond less positively to the speaker.
    B) take the speaker more seriously.
    C) be more objective in responding to the speaker.
    D) do all of the above.

37. A speaker who uses the scanning technique often employs the "rule of three," which involves
    A) a technique similar to "pick six."
    B) focusing on the three nearest listeners.
    C) choosing three audience members to focus on in three different areas of the room.
    D) reiterating the main points three times during the speech.

38. Which nonverbal behavior is most important in maintaining the quality of directness in speech delivery?
    A) eye contact
    B) smiling
    C) gestures
    D) stance

39. Listeners perceive a speaker who slouches as
    A) sloppy, weak, and unfocused.
    B) unqualified yet friendly.
    C) casual and credible.
    D) both A and B.

40. The first thing an audience notices about a speaker approaching the speaking position is his or her
    A) eye contact.
    B) smile.
    C) clothing.
    D) hairstyle.

41. Which of the following may distract listeners?
    A) the color red
    B) dark-colored suits
    C) flashy jewelry
    D) all of the above

42. The display of emotions in a speech should be guided by the social rules of
    A) the culture.
    B) ethics.
    C) oral communication.
    D) the speech setting.

43. The color yellow for a speaker's clothing conveys
    A) a businesslike attitude.
    B) credibility.
    C) friendliness.
    D) formality.

44. A speaker should avoid using ______ when rehearsing the speech.
    A) a watch
    B) a video recorder
    C) a tape recorder
    D) none of the above

45. Videotaping ______ practice sessions is most helpful to a speaker.
    A) two
    B) four
    C) five
    D) at least six

46. When rehearsing a speech, the speaker should
    A) revise the speaking outline.
    B) practice under realistic conditions.
    C) time the speech.
    D) do all of the above.

47. In sum, a speaker should practice a speech at least ______ times in its final form.
    A) two
    B) three
    C) four
    D) five

FILL-IN-THE-BLANK QUESTIONS

48. _______ refers to how something is said, not to what is said.

49. According to one study, listeners may derive only _______ percent of a message's meaning from the words a speaker uses.

50. Nonverbal communication helps establish speaker _______.

51. Audience members respond _______ to speakers whom they perceive to be well dressed and attractive.

52. _______ is an effective tool for a speaker to build rapport with an audience.

53. _______ is probably the most important nonverbal behavior in public speaking.

54. _______ is a technique used by speakers whereby they briefly gaze at all members of the audience.

55. A speaker's _______ should arise from genuine emotions and should conform to the speaker's personality.

56. Gestures have different meanings in different _______.

57. _______ is vital to effective delivery.

58. A speaker who focuses on the _______ makes the speech delivery more natural and confident.

59. Practicing a speech in front of _______ is usually a helpful way for a speaker to rehearse a speech.

60. After rehearsing aloud, a speaker will often revise the _______ outline.

61. The introduction and conclusion should make up no more than _______ percent of the entire speech.

62. Speaking experts recommend practicing a speech about _______ times in its final form.

ESSAY AND SHORT ANSWER QUESTIONS

63. Why are audiences so highly attuned to a speaker's nonverbal communication?

64. Explain why a speaker should always avoid a deadpan facial expression.

65. List two tips for using effective facial expressions.

66. List and explain ways that a speaker can maintain eye contact with the audience.

67. How do a speaker's gestures clarify the speech message?

68. List two tips for effective gesturing.

69. Why should a speaker avoid standing stiffly behind the podium?

70. Explain why a speaker should be aware of variations in nonverbal communication patterns in different cultures.

71. What is the best type of attire for a speaker?

72. List two guidelines for a speaker's dress code.

73. Give three ways that a speaker should practice a speech.

74. Why should a speaker revise the speaking outline after practicing the speech?

75. Why should a speaker time the speech?

ANSWER KEY FOR CHAPTER 19

1. True (p. 267)
2. False (p. 267)
3. True (p. 267)
4. True (p. 267)
5. False (p. 267)
6. True (p. 267)
7. True (p. 268)
8. True (p. 268)
9. False (p. 268)
10. True (p. 268)
11. False (p. 268)
12. False (p. 269)
13. True (p. 269)
14. False (p. 269)
15. False (p. 269)
16. True (p. 270)
17. True (p. 270)
18. True (p. 271)
19. False (p. 271)
20. True (p. 272)
21. False (p. 273)
22. False (p. 273)
23. True (p. 273)
24. True (p. 274)
25. False (pp. 273–274)
26. True (p. 275)
27. False (p. 274)
28. False (p. 274)
29. True (p. 274)
30. True (p. 275)
31. D (p. 267)
32. C (p. 267)
33. A (p. 268)
34. D (p. 268)
35. C (p. 268)
36. A (p. 268)
37. C (p. 270)
38. A (p. 270)
39. A (p. 271)
40. C (p. 271)
41. C (p. 271)
42. A (p. 272)
43. C (p. 271)
44. D (pp. 273–274)
45. A (p. 274)
46. D (p. 274)
47. D (p. 275)
48. Paralanguage (p. 267)
49. 7 (p. 267)
50. credibility (p. 267)
51. positively (p. 268)
52. Smiling (p. 269)
53. Eye contact (p. 269)
54. Scanning (p. 270)
55. gestures (p. 270)
56. cultures (p. 272)
57. Practice (p. 273)
58. message (p. 273)
59. another person (p. 274)
60. speaking (p. 274)
61. 10 to 15 (p. 274)
62. five (p. 275)
63. (No answer, p. 267)
64. (No answer, p. 269)
65. (No answer, p. 269)
66. (No answer, pp. 269–270)
67. (No answer, p. 270)
68. (No answer, p. 270)
69. (No answer, p. 271)
70. (No answer, p. 272)
71. (No answer, p. 271)
72. (No answer, p. 271)
73. (No answer, p. 275)
74. (No answer, p. 274)
75. (No answer, p. 274)

Using Presentation Aids in the Speech 20

TRUE/FALSE QUESTIONS

1. Messages that are visually reinforced are no more believable than those that are only verbalized.

2. Objects, models, pictures, graphs, charts, video, audio, and multimedia can all be used as presentation aids.

3. The strength of a presentation aid lies in the context in which it is used.

4. Research indicates that people remember about 20 percent of what they hear but more than 50 percent of what they see and hear.

5. Presentation aids should serve as the main source of a speaker's ideas.

6. Presentation aids allow listeners to engage the left side of the brain, the hemisphere that plays an important role in verbal tasks.

7. Statistical relationships can be communicated more efficiently and effectively through graphs and charts than through verbal description.

8. A fifteen- to thirty-second video clip is likely to convey about the same amount of information as fifteen to thirty seconds of verbal explanation.

9. A bad presentation aid can tarnish a speaker's image of professionalism.

10. Using an actual object—like a snake or a stone—as a presentation aid can help capture the audience's attention and illustrate key points.

11. A prop is a three-dimensional, scale-size representation of an object.

12. Both diagrams and maps accomplish the same purpose when used as presentation aids.

13. A model is a two-dimensional representation of an object.

14. Posters are a good choice for speakers who give the same presentation many times because they are economical and easy to use

15. Line graphs are useful in representing information that changes over time.

16. A pie graph uses bars of varying lengths to compare quantities or magnitudes.

17. To show the sequence of activities or the directional flow in a process, the pictogram is the visual aid of choice.

18. An organizational chart illustrates the organizational structure or chain of command in an organization.

19. Video can be a powerful presentation aid combining sight, sound, and movement to illustrate key speech concepts.

20. Multimedia combines several media into a single production.

21. The use of multimedia helps people learn and master information more quickly than they would by conventional means.

22. Generating and designing presentation aids by hand is a more popular choice for contemporary speakers than is using the computer.

23. One disadvantage of using overhead transparencies is that they must be shown in a darkened room.

24. Video is one of the most common presentation media.

25. Projection devices that use LCD technology for displaying information come in two forms: the LCD panel and the LCD projector.

26. Video projectors, LCD panels, and LCD projectors are excellent technological presentation aids for large audiences.

27. A chalkboard is a practical presentation aid for a speaker who wants to demonstrate simple explanations.

28. Flip charts are good presentation aids for speakers with few artistic skills.

29. Handouts used for presentation aids should always be passed out before a speech begins.

MULTIPLE-CHOICE QUESTIONS

30. Research findings indicate that people remember about ______ percent of what they hear but more than 50 percent of what they see and hear.
    A) 10
    B) 15
    C) 20
    D) 25

31. Presentation aids should be appropriate to
    A) the audience.
    B) the speech content.
    C) the occasion.
    D) all of the above.

32. Presentation aids
    A) tend to distract audiences.
    B) concisely convey information.
    C) make the speaker seem amateurish.
    D) do all of the above.

33. In Russell's speech about his hobby as an amateur taxidermist, he exhibited several mounted animals as his presentation aids. Which type of presentation aid did Russell use?
    A) models
    B) props
    C) pictograms
    D) handouts

34. Pictures as presentation aids include
    A) diagrams.
    B) graphs.
    C) charts.
    D) models.

35. Which type of graph is useful for presenting information that changes over time?
    A) bar graph
    B) line graph
    C) pie graph
    D pictogram

36. In her speech about divorce rates, Geneva wanted to show a comparison of divorce rates among three states. In order to best illustrate these comparisons, Geneva used a
    A) bar graph.
    B) flowchart.
    C) pie graph.
    D) pictogram.

37. Which type of chart illustrates the sequence of activities or the directional flow in a process?
    A) flowchart
    B) organizational chart
    C) pictogram
    D) table

38. Linda's speech focused on the chain of command within her department. To best demonstrate the communication networks among the employees, Linda used which type of chart?
    A) flowchart
    B) organizational chart
    C) pictogram
    D) table

39. When constructing a pictogram, the speaker should be sure to
    A) select pictures that are different from one another.
    B) make sure the pictures contrast in size and shape.
    C) make certain that the pictorial representation will be understood by viewers.
    D) do all of the above.

40. When using audio or video as a presentation aid, the speaker should be sure to
    A) check to see if the material is copyrighted.
    B) cue the tape before the presentation.

C) tell the audience what they will hear or see beforehand and discuss its significance afterward.
D) do all of the above.

41. As a presentation aid, multimedia
A) cannot yet utilize the Internet.
B) currently has only two presentation graphics programs from which to choose.
C) helps visual but not auditory reinforcement of information.
D) is more time-consuming to prepare than conventional presentation aids.

42. Chalkboards are effective presentation aids when the speaker
A) is unprepared.
B) is explaining an elaborate process or procedure.
C) gives an impromptu explanation.
D) all of the above.

43. To minimize listener distractions, a speaker should
A) distribute handouts at the beginning of the speech.
B) distribute handouts in the middle of the speech.
C) distribute handouts when he/she is finished talking.
D) tell the audience where they can pick up handouts after the speech.

FILL-IN-THE-BLANK QUESTIONS

44. ______ aids are visual or auditory elements used by a speaker that include objects, models, pictures, graphs, charts, video, audio, and multimedia.

45. A(n) ______ is a three-dimensional, scale-size representation of an object.

46. A(n) ______ represents numerical data in visual form.

47. A diagram that shows a step-by-step progression through a procedure, relationship, or process is called a(n) ______.

48. A(n) ______ graph uses columns of various lengths to compare quantities or magnitudes.

49. When creating a graph, a speaker should put no more than ______ lines of data on one graph.

50. A graph should always be assigned a clear ______.

51. When creating a pie graph, the number of pie slices should be restricted to ______.

52. Video- and audio-______ are reusable, which makes this medium both durable and cost-effective.

53. A presentation aid that combines several media (such as voice, video, text, and data) into a single production is called ______.

54. An LCD ______ is a device with its own light source that allows a speaker to project what is on a computer screen.

55. Page-size items conveying information that is impractical to give in another manner or that is kept by listeners after the presentation are called ______.

ESSAY AND SHORT ANSWER QUESTIONS

56. Why should presentation aids supplement or enhance the speech rather than serve as the main source of the speaker's ideas?

57. How can speaker credibility be affected by the use or misuse of presentation aids?

58. List two ways that presentation aids may backfire or create an unprofessional image for the speaker.

59. Choose two types of pictures (photographs, drawings, diagrams, maps, or posters) and define each; then explain a speech topic for which these presentation aids would be appropriate.

60. Explain the difference between a line graph and a bar graph.

61. When would a pictogram be more suitable than a bar graph for a presentation aid?

62. What is a pie graph, and when would it be appropriate for use as a presentation aid?

63. Explain and give an example of a flowchart, an organizational chart, and a table.

64. How can an audio or video clip enhance a speaker's main points?

65. List two advantages of slide and overhead transparencies.

66. Describe an advantage of computer-generated graphics.

67. When would a flip chart be more suitable than a chalkboard for a presentation aid?

68. Identify two advantages and two disadvantages of handouts as a presentation aid.

ANSWER KEY FOR CHAPTER 20

1. False (p. 282)
2. True (p. 282)
3. True (p. 282)
4. True (p. 282)
5. False (p. 282)
6. False (p. 282)
7. True (p. 283)
8. False (p. 283)
9. True (p. 283)
10. True (p. 283)
11. False (p. 283)
12. False (p. 284)
13. False (p. 283)
14. True (p. 286)
15. True (p. 286)
16. False (p. 286)
17. False (p. 288)
18. True (p. 288)
19. True (p. 290)
20. True (p. 291)
21. True (p. 291)
22. False (p. 292)
23. False (p. 292)
24. False (p. 291)
25. True (p. 292)
26. True (p. 293)
27. True (p. 294)
28. False (p. 294)
29. False (p. 294)
30. C (p. 282)
31. D (p. 283)
32. B (p. 283)
33. B (p. 283)
34. A (p. 284)
35. B (p. 286)
36. A (p. 286)
37. A (p. 288)
38. B (p. 288)
39. C (p. 287)
40. D (p. 290)
41. D (p. 291)
42. C (p. 294)
43. C (p. 294)
44. Presentation (p. 282)
45. model (p. 283)
46. graph (p. 286)
47. flowchart (p. 288)
48. bar (p. 286)
49. two (p. 289)
50. title (p. 289)
51. seven (p. 289)
52. tapes (p. 290)
53. multimedia (p. 291)
54. projector (p. 292)
55. handouts (p. 294)
56. (No answer, p. 282)
57. (No answer, p. 283)
58. (No answer, pp. 283–284)
59. (No answer, pp. 284–286)
60. (No answer, p. 286)
61. (No answer, p. 287)
62. (No answer, pp. 286–287)
63. (No answer, pp. 288–290)
64. (No answer, p. 290)
65. (No answer, p. 291)
66. (No answer, p. 292)
67. (No answer, p. 294)
68. (No answer, p. 294)

Designing Presentation Aids 21

TRUE/FALSE QUESTIONS

1. The purpose of a presentation aid is to reinforce, support, or summarize the speaker's words.

2. A presentation aid with words should have no more than eight words per line.

3. A presentation aid with words should have no more than five lines per aid.

4. Key design elements such as fonts, color, and italics should be consistent with each presentation aid to maintain continuity.

5. Presentation aids that try to communicate too many messages will overwhelm the audience.

6. Limiting the number of words in a presentation aid increases the likelihood that the audience will spend too much time reading the aid rather than listening to the speaker.

7. Each presentation aid should be simple and uncomplicated and should present three major ideas per aid.

8. The word *fonts* refers to a specific style of lettering.

9. Sans serif typefaces include small flourishes, or strokes, at the tops and bottoms of each letter.

10. Boldface, underlining, and italics should be used sparingly to call attention to the most important points.

11. Presentation aids are most effective when the words are written in all uppercase letters.

12. For on-screen projection, a speaker should not use a font smaller than 18-point text.

13. Typefaces can be purchased in separate software packages or downloaded from the Internet.

14. For on-screen projection, titles or major headings should be 36-point text.

15. For on-screen projection, regular text should be 12-point type.

16. Colors evoke distinct associations in people.

17. Bold, bright colors should be used to emphasize important points.

18. Different audiences may assign different meanings to particular colors.

19. Avoid dark colors for presentation aid backgrounds.

20. Presentation aids that use four or more colors are more effective than those that use only two or three.

21. When using color, stay within the same family of hues.

MULTIPLE-CHOICE QUESTIONS

22. How many major ideas should be present in each presentation aid?
    A) one
    B) two
    C) three
    D) four

23. When designing a presentation aid, the speaker should strive for
    A) simplicity.
    B) abstraction.
    C) complexity.
    D) diversity.

24. Typefaces come in a variety of sizes or
    A) scripts.
    B) sans scripts.
    C) fonts.
    D) serifs.

25. The two categories of typefaces are sans serif and
    A) script.
    B) sans script.
    C) font.
    D) serif.

26. When the body of a text is being read, which typeface is easiest on the eye?
    A) script
    B) sans script
    C) font
    D) serif

27. Small amounts of text, such as headings, are best viewed in which type?
    A) script
    B) sans script
    C) sans serif
    D) serif

28. The typeface or font in a presentation should
    A) be simple.
    B) be in all capitals.
    C) be ornate.
    D) include multiple types of typeface.

29. Boldface, underlining, and italics should
    A) be used as often as possible.
    B) emphasize both major and minor points.
    C) be used sparingly.
    D) both A and B.

30. The skillful use of color in presentation aids can be used to
    A) draw attention to key points.
    B) set the mood of a speech.
    C) do both A and B.
    D) do neither A nor B.

31. Speakers often use which color to draw attention to important points?
    A) blue
    B) yellow
    C) green
    D) black

32. To de-emphasize less important areas of a presentation, use
    A) red.
    B) smaller font.
    C) italics.
    D) light colors.

33. The background color of a presentation aid
    A) should be dark.
    B) should have several hues.
    C) should be neutral in color.
    D) should blend into the type.

FILL-IN-THE-BLANK QUESTIONS

34. The principle of ______ states that it is appropriate to present one major idea per aid.

35. The principle of ______ dictates that the same design should apply to all presentation aids displayed in a speech.

36. The purpose of ______ is to reinforce, support, or summarize the speaker's words.

37. A presentation aid with words should have no more than ______ words per line.

38. Key design elements such as fonts, color, and italics should be consistent with each presentation aid to maintain ______.

39. Presentation aids that try to communicate too many messages will overwhelm the ______.

40. Limiting the number of ______ in a presentation aid lessens the likelihood that the audience will spend too much time reading the aid rather than listening to the speaker.

41. Different sizes of typefaces are called ______.

42. The word ______ refers to a specific style of lettering.

43. For on-screen projection, titles or major headings should be ______ type size.

44. For on-screen projection, regular text should be ______ type size.

45. Different cultures may attach different meanings to particular _______.

ESSAY AND SHORT ANSWER QUESTIONS

46. Why should speakers use phrases rather than full sentences in presentation aids?

47. How many major ideas should be presented in each presentation aid? Why?

48. Explain the principles of simplicity and continuity, and give an example of each.

49. Give three tips for using typefaces and fonts effectively in a presentation aid.

50. Explain why text in a presentation aid should appear in upper- and lowercase type rather than in all uppercase.

51. List four ways to optimize color in designing presentation aids.

ANSWER KEY FOR CHAPTER 21

1. True (p. 295)
2. True (p. 295)
3. False (p. 295)
4. True (p. 296)
5. True (p. 295)
6. False (p. 295)
7. False (p. 295)
8. False (p. 297)
9. False (p. 297)
10. True (p. 298)
11. False (p. 298)
12. True (p. 298)
13. True (p. 298)
14. True (p. 298)
15. False (p. 298)
16. True (p. 299)
17. True (p. 300)
18. True (p. 300)
19. True (p. 300)
20. False (p. 300)
21. True (p. 300)
22. A (p. 295)
23. A (p. 295)
24. C (p. 297)
25. D (p. 297)
26. D (p. 297)
27. C (p. 298)
28. D (p. 298)
29. C (p. 298)
30. C (p. 299)
31. B (p. 300)
32. D (p. 298)
33. C (p. 300)
34. simplicity (p. 295)
35. continuity (p. 296)
36. presentation aids (p. 295)
37. eight (p. 295)
38. continuity (p. 297)
39. audience (p. 295)
40. words (p. 295)
41. fonts (p. 297)
42. typeface (p. 297)
43. 36-point (p. 298)
44. 18-point (p. 298)
45. colors (p. 300)
46. (No answer, p. 295)
47. (No answer, p. 295)
48. (No answer, pp. 295–297)
49. (No answer, pp. 297–299)
50. (No answer, p. 298)
51. (No answer, p. 300)

22 *Using Presentation Software*

TRUE/FALSE QUESTIONS

1. Presentation software packages offer public speakers powerful tools for creating and displaying professionally polished visual aids.
2. Presentation software allows the user to import video and sound for a multimedia presentation.
3. Presentation software programs give users the ability to modify and revise the aids up to the minute the speech is delivered.
4. Creating aids with presentation software is effortless.
5. Learning to use a presentation software program is quick and easy.
6. Speakers who rely on electronic presentations risk performance difficulties due to technical errors.
7. One potential disadvantage of electronic presentations is the temptation to focus on the aids rather than on the speech.
8. A speaker's primary mission is to communicate through a showy multimedia program rather than through the spoken word.
9. Some speakers are inclined to hide behind their presentation aids, focusing on the aids rather than on the audience.
10. In a speech with multimedia, the presentation aids should be the primary focus, with the audience and the message being secondary.
11. Since most computer systems are similar, speakers should not worry too much about familiarizing themselves with the layout and functioning of the presentation computer prior to delivering the speech.
12. It is a good idea for speakers to prepare a hard-copy backup of an electronic presentation.
13. Popular presentation programs on the market today include both Microsoft PowerPoint and Adobe PhotoShop.
14. With PowerPoint, a speaker can generate slides containing text, artwork, and photos but not video or sound.

15. In PowerPoint, a touch screen allows quick access to the most frequently used program functions.

16. After launching PowerPoint, the program displays a blank slide with options for creating a new presentation or opening and revising an existing one.

17. In PowerPoint, transition effects add special motion and sound effects as the user moves from one slide to another.

18. Animation effects are also referred to as *builds.*

19. PowerPoint 2000 comes with either Preset or Custom animations.

20. With PowerPoint, clip art cannot be imported from other online programs.

21. Charts can be automatically inserted into a PowerPoint slide.

22. With PowerPoint 2000, the user can create worksheets, but not tables, within the program.

23. Technology should not get in the way of a speaker's relating to the audience.

MULTIPLE-CHOICE QUESTIONS

24. Technical errors that can arise from using presentation software include
    A) files that won't open.
    B) files that are not properly saved to disk.
    C) incompatible versions of software.
    D) all of the above.

25. Which of the following options does PowerPoint offer for creating a new presentation?
    A) AutoFixer
    B) AutoContent Wizard
    C) AutoPlanning
    D) all of the above

26. Which of the following PowerPoint options offers the greatest degree of help?
    A) AutoContent Wizard
    B) Template option
    C) Blank Presentation option
    D) Guidebook Pattern

27. Which of the following PowerPoint options is best for speakers who want more flexibility in designing their graphics?
    A) AutoContent Wizard
    B) Template option
    C) Blank Presentation option
    D) Guidebook Pattern

28. Which of the following PowerPoint options allows the user to organize points and subpoints?
    A) AutoContent Wizard
    B) Design Template option
    C) Blank Presentation option
    D) Guidebook Pattern

29. In which mode of PowerPoint do users customize every aspect of the presentation?
    A) AutoContent Wizard
    B) Template option
    C) Blank Presentation option
    D) Guidebook Pattern

30. Which of the following PowerPoint options allows the greatest degree of creativity and flexibility?
    A) AutoContent Wizard
    B) Template option
    C) Blank Presentation option
    D) Guidebook Pattern

31. Which view in PowerPoint allows the user to look at one entire slide on the screen and edit it?
    A) normal view
    B) outline view
    C) slide sorter view
    D) slide show view

32. Which view in PowerPoint provides a graphical representation of all the slides in the presentation?
    A) slide view
    B) outline view
    C) slide sorter view
    D) slide show view

33. Which view in PowerPoint is meant to be used during projection to an audience?
    A) slide view
    B) outline view
    C) slide sorter view
    D) slide show view

34. Used sparingly, which of the following PowerPoint effects can add to the effectiveness of a presentation?
    A) transitions
    B) animations
    C) both A and B
    D) neither A nor B

35. Which of the following can be inserted into PowerPoint slides?
    A) clip art
    B) charts
    C) tables and worksheets
    D) all of the above

FILL-IN-THE-BLANK QUESTIONS

36. Presentation software allows the user to import video and sound for a(n) ______ presentation.

37. Speakers who rely on electronic presentations risk performance difficulties due to ______ errors.

38. One potential disadvantage of electronic presentations is the temptation to focus on the aids rather than on the ______.

39. Speakers should familiarize themselves with the layout and functioning of the presentation ______ prior to delivering the speech.

40. It is a good idea for speakers to prepare a(n) ______ backup of an electronic presentation.

41. The three options for creating a new presentation in PowerPoint are ______, ______, and ______.

42. Newer versions of PowerPoint provide ______ different ways to view the aids created by the user rather than the previous five ways.

43. For every graphic the user creates, PowerPoint creates a set of ______.

44. In PowerPoint, ______ effects add special motion and sound effects as the user moves from one slide to another.

45. Animation effects are also referred to as ______.

46. When making hard copies of your PowerPoint presentation, there are ______ options for output format.

ESSAY AND SHORT ANSWER QUESTIONS

47. How can a speaker avoid hiding behind an electronic presentation?

48. Aids created from presentation software are easy to generate. Explain how this ease of use can be problematic.

49. Why should speakers familiarize themselves with the equipment they will use during the actual speech?

50. How can a speaker prepare for the potential incompatibilities between software versions?

51. Identify three components of PowerPoint's AutoContent Wizard option.

52. Under what circumstances might a speaker choose PowerPoint's Template option for designing presentation aids?

53. When should a speaker choose PowerPoint's Blank Presentation option?

54. Explain how PowerPoint's "masters" aid the speaker in preparing presentation aids.

55. Define *animation effects* and explain their use in PowerPoint.

56. List three objects that can be created or imported into PowerPoint slides.

57. Give three tips for successfully incorporating electronic presentations into a speech.

ANSWER KEY FOR CHAPTER 22

1. True (p. 301)
2. True (p. 301)
3. True (p. 301)
4. False (p. 301)
5. False (p. 301)
6. True (p. 301)
7. True (p. 302)
8. False (p. 302)
9. True (p. 302)
10. False (p. 302)
11. False (p. 302)
12. True (p. 302)
13. False (p. 302)
14. False (p. 302)
15. False (p. 304)
16. True (p. 303)
17. True (p. 308)
18. True (p. 308)
19. False (p. 309)
20. False (p. 310)
21. True (p. 310)
22. False (p. 311)
23. True (p. 314)
24. D (p. 301)
25. B (p. 304)
26. A (p. 304)
27. B (p. 304)
28. B (p. 305)
29. C (p. 306)
30. C (p. 306)
31. A (p. 306)
32. C (p. 307)
33. D (p. 307)
34. C (p. 308)
35. D (p. 310)
36. multimedia (p. 301)
37. technical (p. 301)
38. speech (p. 302)
39. computer (p. 302)
40. hard-copy (p. 302)
41. AutoContent Wizard; Template option; Blank Presentation option (p. 304)
42. three (p. 306)
43. masters (p. 307)
44. transition (p. 308)
45. builds (p. 308)
46. four (p. 312)
47. (No answer, p. 302)
48. (No answer, p. 302)
49. (No answer, p. 302)
50. (No answer, p. 302)
51. (No answer, p. 304)
52. (No answer, pp. 304–305)
53. (No answer, p. 306)
54. (No answer, p. 307)
55. (No answer, p. 308)
56. (No answer, p. 310)
57. (No answer, p. 314)

54. Information that challenges accepted ways of thinking about things is called a(n) ______.

55. Explanations that link the unfamiliar with the familiar often take the form of a(n) ______.

ESSAY AND SHORT ANSWER QUESTIONS

56. List three ways a speaker can build audience awareness and understanding in an informative speech.

57. How can a speaker gauge the informational needs of the audience?

58. Name three ways that a speaker can define information, and give an example of each.

59. How is explaining information different from describing information?

60. Provide an example of a speech topic that would be appropriate for demonstrating information.

61. List the subject matter categories of informative speeches.

62. List three guidelines for presenting effective informative speeches.

ANSWER KEY FOR CHAPTER 23

1. False (p. 327)
2. True (p. 328)
3. True (p. 327)
4. False (p. 328)
5. False (p. 329)
6. True (p. 329)
7. False (p. 329)
8. False (p. 333)
9. True (p. 332)
10. False (p. 333)
11. False (p. 333)
12. False (p. 333)
13. True (p. 333)
14. False (p. 334)
15. True (p. 333)
16. True (p. 330)
17. False (p. 330)
18. False (p. 331)
19. False (p. 328)
20. False (p. 331)
21. False (p. 327)
22. True (p. 335)
23. True (pp. 335–336)
24. False (p. 332)
25. True (p. 338)
26. False (p. 337)
27. D (p. 327)
28. C (p. 327)
29. D (p. 328)
30. A (p. 333)
31. C (p. 332)
32. C (p. 333)
33. A (p. 330)
34. C (p. 330)
35. D (p. 330)
36. B (p. 331)
37. A (p. 331)
38. A (p. 328)
39. C (p. 331)
40. D (p. 330)
41. D (p. 328)
42. A (p. 332)
43. D (p. 334)
44. inform (p. 327)
45. audience (p. 327)
46. negation (p. 332)
47. operational (p. 332)
48. synonym (p. 333)
49. etymology (p. 333)
50. events (p. 330)
51. processes (p. 330)
52. issues (p. 331)
53. persuasive (p. 328)
54. counterintuitive idea (p. 335)
55. analogy (pp. 335–336)
56. (No answer, p. 328)
57. (No answer, p. 329)
58. (No answer, pp. 332–333)
59. (No answer, pp. 333–334)
60. (No answer, p. 333)
61. (No answer, p. 334)
62. (No answer, p. 337)

The Persuasive Speech 24

TRUE/FALSE QUESTIONS

1. The general goal of persuasive speeches is to sway listeners to the speaker's point of view.
2. The persuasive speaker's objective is to limit the audience's alternatives to the side the speaker represents by ignoring unfavorable alternatives altogether.
3. All persuasive speeches explicitly seek a response from the audience.
4. A persuasive speaker should not attempt to reinforce an audience's existing attitudes, beliefs, or behavior.
5. The successful and ethical persuasive speaker acknowledges that audience choices are ultimately made for them by the speaker.
6. The persuader who seeks only minor changes is usually more successful at achieving them than the speaker who seeks major changes.
7. The listeners' feelings toward the speaker do not influence how receptive they will be toward her or his message.
8. A speaker is more likely to persuade audience members whose position differs only moderately from the speaker's.
9. For persuasive change to endure, the audience must be convinced that they will somehow be rewarded.
10. According to Aristotle, rhetorical proof consists of logos, ethos, and mythos.
11. Persuasive appeals directed at the audience's reasoning on a topic are termed *logos.*
12. A three-part argument consisting of a major premise, a minor premise, and a conclusion is called an *enthymeme.*
13. Pathos involves the appeal to audience emotion.
14. To ensure that a speech is ethical, the speaker should evaluate her or his appeal to an audience's emotions on the basis of sound reasoning.
15. Pathos cannot be used in an unethical manner by a speaker.

16. According to Aristotle, appealing to the emotions of the listeners is called *ethos.*

17. One element of an ethos-based appeal is the speaker's moral character.

18. Maslow's hierarchy of needs is a set of ten basic human needs.

19. The highest level in Maslow's hierarchy is self-esteem needs.

20. The elaboration likelihood model is a theory of persuasion that maintains that people consciously evaluate the potential costs and benefits associated with taking a particular action.

21. Central processing occurs when listeners are influenced primarily by the strength and quality of the speaker's arguments.

22. The level of involvement that the audience feels in the speech's message can affect the audience's reactions.

23. Speaker credibility is invoked only in the speaker's message.

24. A speaker's expertise is a more important speaker attribute than a speaker's trustworthiness.

25. Speaker similarity involves listeners' perceptions of how similar the speaker is to themselves, especially in terms of attitudes and moral character.

26. For the most part, speakers who are physically attractive are more successful in accomplishing their persuasive attempts than are unattractive speakers.

MULTIPLE-CHOICE QUESTIONS

27. A persuasive speech
    A) attempts to influence audience choices.
    B) presents listeners with a limited number of alternatives to consider.
    C) seeks a response from the audience.
    D) does all of the above.

28. Under which of the following conditions is the persuasive purpose appropriate?
    A) when you seek to expand an audience's alternatives
    B) when you seek to change an audience's behavior
    C) when you seek to reinforce an audience's attitudes, beliefs, or behavior
    D) both B and C

29. According to Aristotle, rhetorical proof consists of
    A) logos, ethos, and pathos.
    B) logos, mythos, and ethos.
    C) logos, pathos, and mythos.
    D) logos, ethos, and credos.

30. A speaker is more likely to persuade audience members whose position differs _______ from the speaker's.
A) totally
B) moderately
C) drastically
D) ethically

31. A three-part argument consisting of a major premise, a minor premise, and a conclusion is called
A) a syllogism.
B) an enthymeme.
C) an elaboration.
D) central processing.

32. The appeal to audience emotion is termed
A) logos.
B) ethos.
C) pathos.
D) credos.

33. In his persuasive speech about why people should buy used instead of new autos, Maverick provided the audience with convincing information because of his knowledge and experience as a used-car salesperson. Maverick employed which type of appeal?
A) logos
B) ethos
C) pathos
D) credos

34. Buck gave a persuasive speech about why people should assist the homeless in his city in order to prevent crime. According to Maslow, this speech appealed to which basic need?
A) physiological
B) safety
C) social
D) self-esteem

35. In his presentation to his co-workers, Kyle encouraged his colleagues to reach their highest potential and take pride in their work. According to Maslow's hierarchy, which need did Kyle appeal to?
A) physiological
B) social
C) self-esteem
D) self-actualization

36. According to the elaboration likelihood model, more long-lasting changes in audience perspectives occur if listeners process the speech message
A) centrally.
B) peripherally.
C) favorably.
D) diffusively.

37. Although the audience did not pay close attention to Claire's speech message, they were influenced by her professional attire and her reputation as a dedicated social worker. According to the elaboration likelihood model, which of the following swayed the audience to think positively about Claire?
A) central processing
B) marginal processing
C) peripheral processing
D) diffusive processing

38. The audience's perceptions of and attitudes toward a speaker make up the speaker's
    A) expertise.
    B) credibility.
    C) ethos.
    D) persuasiveness.

39. A speaker can enhance her or his credibility with the audience by
    A) preparing well.
    B) demonstrating trustworthiness.
    C) being well groomed.
    D) doing all of the above.

40. Persuasive speech outcomes are strongly influenced by audience perceptions of
    A) speaker expertise and trustworthiness.
    B) speaker attractiveness.
    C) speaker similarity to listeners.
    D) all of the above.

FILL-IN-THE-BLANK QUESTIONS

41. Speech that is intended to influence the beliefs, attitudes, values, and acts of others is called ______ speaking.

42. The general goal of ______ speeches is to increase understanding and awareness.

43. According to Aristotle, the speaker's use of three modes of classical persuasion are forms of ______ proof.

44. A(n) ______ is a three-part argument consisting of a major premise, a minor premise, and a conclusion.

45. A speaker who identifies and appeals to the audience's emotions employs the classical persuasive appeal known as ______.

46. In classical terms, a speaker's moral character is called ______.

47. A contemporary persuasive model used by speakers and formulated by Abraham Maslow is Maslow's hierarchy of ______.

48. The ______ is a theory of persuasion that maintains that people consciously evaluate the potential costs and benefits associated with taking a particular action.

49. ______ is comprised of audience perceptions of and attitudes toward the speaker's perceived expertise, trustworthiness, similarity to audience members, and attractiveness.

ESSAY AND SHORT ANSWER QUESTIONS

50. Explain the persuasive speaker's objective of "limiting the audience's alternatives."

51. Explain two differences between informative and persuasive speeches.

52. Describe two ways in which a speaker can demonstrate to the audience that he or she is an ethical speaker.

53. Explain Richard Petty and John Cacioppo's elaboration likelihood model of persuasion, and discuss central and peripheral processing.

54. How do the listeners' feelings toward the speaker influence how receptive an audience will be toward the speaker's message?

55. Define and briefly explain the terms *logos, ethos,* and *pathos.*

56. Provide an example of a syllogism.

57. How do the audience's perceptions of the speaker's moral character affect the outcome of a persuasive speech?

58. Explain how Maslow's hierarchy of needs relates to persuasive speaking.

59. Explain the elaboration likelihood model, and discuss how this theory of persuasion can be utilized by a persuasive speaker.

60. Why are the audience's perceptions of the speaker's trustworthiness more important than their perceptions of the speaker's expertise?

61. How does the physical attractiveness of the speaker contribute to the overall persuasiveness of the message?

ANSWER KEY FOR CHAPTER 24

1. True (p. 346)
2. False (p. 347)
3. False (p. 347)
4. False (p. 346)
5. False (p. 347)
6. True (p. 348)
7. False (p. 348)
8. True (p. 349)
9. True (p. 349)
10. False (pp. 350–353)
11. True (p. 350)
12. False (p. 350)
13. True (p. 351)
14. True (p. 352)
15. False (p. 352)
16. False (p. 352)
17. True (p. 354)
18. False (p. 355)
19. False (p. 355)
20. False (pp. 356, 358)
21. True (p. 358)
22. True (p. 348)
23. False (pp. 358–360)
24. False (p. 359)
25. True (p. 359)
26. True (p. 360)
27. D (pp. 346–347)
28. D (p. 347)
29. A (pp. 349–354)
30. B (p. 349)
31. A (p. 350)
32. C (p. 351)
33. B (p. 354)
34. B (p. 356)
35. D (p. 356)
36. A (p. 358)
37. C (p. 358)
38. B (p. 358)
39. D (pp. 358–361)
40. D (p. 358)
41. persuasive (p. 346)
42. informative (p. 346)
43. rhetorical (p. 349)
44. syllogism (p. 350)
45. pathos (p. 351)
46. ethos (p. 353)
47. needs (p. 355)
48. expectancy-outcome values theory (p. 356)
49. Credibility (p. 358)
50. (No answer, p. 347)
51. (No answer, pp. 346–347)
52. (No answer, p. 347)
53. (No answer, p. 358)
54. (No answer, pp. 353–354)
55. (No answer, pp. 350–354)
56. (No answer, p. 350)
57. (No answer, p. 354)
58. (No answer, p. 355)
59. (No answer, p. 358)
60. (No answer, p. 359)
61. (No answer, p. 360)

Developing Arguments for the Persuasive Speech 25

TRUE/FALSE QUESTIONS

1. An argument is a stated position with support either for or against an idea or issue.
2. A claim declares some state of affairs and is often presented as a thesis statement.
3. Material that provides grounds for belief in a claim is called *evidence.*
4. A warrant declares some state of affairs, as in a thesis statement.
5. Speculative claims focus on conditions that actually exist or have existed in the past.
6. Claims of value address issues of judgment and try to show why something is right or wrong, good or bad, worthy or unworthy.
7. A claim of value consists of a problem, a solution, and evidence of the solution's feasibility.
8. Claims of policy generally contain the word *should.*
9. Claims of policy advocate change and recommend that a specific course of action be taken.
10. Claims of fact and policy require evidence, whereas claims of value do not.
11. Arguments in a speech should not be built on the basis of the speaker's own knowledge, opinions, and expertise.
12. External evidence can be thought of as supporting material.
13. Narratives, testimony, and facts drawn from an outside source are examples of external evidence.
14. Usually, motivational warrants are implied rather than stated outright.
15. The success or failure of authoritative warrants relies on how highly the audience regards the authority figure.
16. Motivational warrants operate on the basis of credibility attributed to the source of evidence.

17. Warrants by cause operate on the basis of audience needs and emotions.

18. Authoritative warrants operate on the basis of credibility attributed to the source of evidence.

19. Substantive warrants operate on the basis of an audience's beliefs about the reliability of factual evidence.

20. Warrants by sign compare two similar cases and infer that what is true in one is true in the other.

21. The inoculation effect is a theory that contends that a speaker can "inoculate" an audience against counterarguments by anticipating and addressing or rebutting them.

22. If the audience is aware of counterarguments and the speaker fails to address them, the speaker risks losing credibility with the audience.

23. A fallacy takes the form of a false statement or an invalid line of reasoning.

24. Using a circular thought pattern, begging the question is a fallacy that states a claim in an impressive manner but really has no substance at all.

25. Bandwagoning is a fallacy that assigns a claim greater substance by making it appear more popular than it really is.

26. *Everyone wears Adidas* is an example of begging the question.

27. Ad hominem arguments attack the person's argument rather than the person making the argument.

28. The either-or fallacy poses an argument in terms of only two alternatives.

29. Understanding different types of fallacies is not an important concern for listeners.

MULTIPLE-CHOICE QUESTIONS

30. In persuasive speaking, arguments are created to
    A) change people's opinions.
    B) influence behavior.
    C) justify the speaker's beliefs or actions.
    D) do all of the above.

31. An argument consists of
    A) a claim, opinions, and a conclusion.
    B) a claim, evidence, and warrants.
    C) a claim, fallacies, and opinions.
    D) a claim, warrants, and a conclusion.

32. A claim is also called
   A) a proposition.
   B) a policy.
   C) a value.
   D) all of the above.

33. *The Chicago Bulls were the winningest NBA team of the 1990s.* This statement is a claim of
   A) value.
   B) fact.
   C) policy.
   D) none of the above.

34. *The Chicago Bulls were the best NBA team of the 1990s.* This statement is a claim of
   A) value.
   B) fact.
   C) policy.
   D) none of the above.

35. *Students who earn an A average on all speech assignments should be exempt from the final exam.* This statement is a claim of
   A) value.
   B) fact.
   C) policy.
   D) none of the above.

36. To build a strong case for a claim of ______, the speaker must provide the audience with a three-part justification consisting of a need or problem, a solution, and evidence of the solution's feasibility.
   A) value
   B) fact
   C) policy
   D) third order

37. The most persuasive kind of evidence is
   A) the audience's knowledge and opinions about the topic.
   B) the speaker's assertions based on personal experience and knowledge.
   C) information from external sources, such as testimony and statistics.
   D) none of the above.

38. The second most persuasive kind of evidence is
   A) the audience's knowledge and opinions about the topic.
   B) the speaker's assertions based on personal experience and knowledge.
   C) information from external sources, such as testimony and statistics.
   D) none of the above.

39. Warrants that appeal to the audience's emotions are called ______ warrants.
   A) speculative
   B) motivational
   C) authoritative
   D) substantive

40. Warrants that rely on an audience's beliefs about the credibility or acceptability of a source of evidence are termed ______ warrants.
   A) speculative
   B) motivational
   C) authoritative
   D) substantive

41. ______ warrants appeal to the audience's reasoning.
   A) Speculative
   B) Motivational
   C) Authoritative
   D) Substantive

42. A warrant that compares two similar cases and infers that what is true in one is true in the other is a
    A) warrant by sign.
    B) warrant by analogy.
    C) warrant by cause.
    D) warrant by evidence.

43. A speaker who anticipates counterarguments and then addresses or refutes them uses
    A) authoritative warrants.
    B) fallacies.
    C) speculative claims.
    D) the inoculation effect.

44. From an ethical perspective, a speaker may ignore counterclaims if
    A) they severely weaken the speaker's arguments.
    B) the speaker does not have time to address them adequately.
    C) the audience is at least vaguely aware of the counterclaims.
    D) all of the above are true.

45. *I should be paid $50 for mowing the lawn because this lawn is worth $50.* This statement is an example of
    A) begging the question.
    B) bandwagoning.
    C) overgeneralization.
    D) ad hominem argument.

46. *Cheating on an exam is not unusual. After all, most college students cheat on an exam at least once.* These statements are an example of
    A) begging the question.
    B) bandwagoning.
    C) overgeneralization.
    D) ad hominem argument.

47. *We should disregard Steven Bryan's ideas concerning muscle cars because Steven Bryan is an idiot.* This statement is an example of
    A) begging the question.
    B) bandwagoning.
    C) overgeneralization.
    D) ad hominem argument.

FILL-IN-THE-BLANK QUESTIONS

48. A(n) ______ is a stated position with support either for or against an idea or issues.

49. A(n) ______ is a statement that provides a logical connection between some evidence and a claim.

50. Claims of ______ focus on conditions that actually exist, existed in the past, or will exist in the future.

51. Claims of ______ address issues of judgment and try to show why something is right or wrong, good or bad, worthy or unworthy.

52. ______ evidence is any information in support of a claim that originates with sources other than the audience or the speaker.

53. The key to using an audience's knowledge and opinions to support your claim is ______.

54. Nothing is more ______ to listeners than a reaffirmation of their own attitudes, beliefs, and values.

55. Warrants by ______ compare two similar cases and infer that what is true in one is true in the other.

56. A false or erroneous statement, or an invalid or deceptive line of reasoning is called a logical ______.

57. An attack on the opponent instead of on the opponent's arguments is called a(n) ______ argument.

ESSAY AND SHORT ANSWER QUESTIONS

58. Why is it important for a speaker to understand how to construct an argument?

59. Explain the differences among a claim, a warrant, and evidence.

60. Give an example of a claim of value.

61. Give an example of a claim of policy.

62. Provide three examples of external evidence.

63. List and explain the three tests of evidence.

64. Give an example of how warrants sometimes rely on an audience's beliefs about the credibility of a source of evidence.

65. Explain the difference between a motivational warrant and an authoritative warrant.

66. Explain the difference between a warrant by sign and a warrant by cause.

67. Define *warrant by analogy.*

68. Describe how a speaker can use the inoculation effect in a persuasive speech.

69. List two reasons why it is important to be able to identify fallacious reasoning.

70. Give an example of the logical fallacy called begging the question.

71. Give an example of an either-or fallacy.

72. Give an example of an ad hominem argument.

ANSWER KEY FOR CHAPTER 25

1. True (p. 361)
2. True (p. 361)
3. True (p. 362)
4. False (p. 362)
5. False (p. 365)
6. True (p. 365)
7. False (p. 366)
8. True (p. 365)
9. True (p. 365)
10. False (p. 365)
11. False (p. 367)
12. True (p. 368)
13. True (p. 368)
14. True (pp. 369–370)
15. True (p. 370)
16. False (p. 370)
17. False (p. 371)
18. True (p. 370)
19. True (p. 371)
20. False (p. 371)
21. True (p. 373)
22. True (p. 373)
23. True (p. 373)
24. True (pp. 373–374)
25. True (p. 374)
26. False (p. 374)
27. False (p. 374)
28. True (p. 374)
29. False (p. 373)
30. D (p. 361)
31. B (p. 361)
32. A (p. 361)
33. B (p. 364)
34. A (p. 365)
35. C (p. 365)
36. C (p. 366)
37. A (p. 367)
38. B (p. 367)
39. B (p. 370)
40. C (p. 370)
41. D (p. 371)
42. B (p. 372)
43. D (p. 373)
44. B (p. 373)
45. A (pp. 373–374)
46. B (p. 374)
47. D (p. 374)
48. argument (p. 361)
49. warrant (p. 362)
50. fact (p. 364)
51. value (p. 365)
52. External (p. 368)
53. audience analysis (p. 367)
54. persuasive (p. 368)
55. analogy (p. 372)
56. fallacy (p. 373)
57. ad hominem (p. 374)
58. (No answer, p. 361)
59. (No answer, pp. 361–363)
60. (No answer, p. 365)
61. (No answer, p. 365)
62. (No answer, pp. 368–369)
63. (No answer, p. 368)
64. (No answer, p. 367)
65. (No answer, pp. 369–370)
66. (No answer, p. 371)
67. (No answer, p. 372)
68. (No answer, p. 373)
69. (No answer, p. 373)
70. (No answer, pp. 373–374)
71. (No answer, p. 374)
72. (No answer, p. 374)

Organizing the Persuasive Speech 26

TRUE/FALSE QUESTIONS

1. The nature of the audience is an important factor to consider when selecting your organizational pattern.

2. The nature of your arguments and evidence is not an important factor to consider when selecting your organizational pattern.

3. Claims of policy fit naturally into the problem-solution pattern.

4. The cause-effect pattern of organization arranges main points to demonstrate a series of advantages associated with the speaker's claim.

5. The organizational pattern that can soften the reservations of a hostile audience is the refutation pattern of organization.

6. A sympathetic audience is the same as an apathetic audience.

7. The specific speech purpose is a factor to consider when deciding on speech organization.

8. The problem-solution pattern does not, in fact, always require the presentation of a solution.

9. There are four steps in Monroe's motivated sequence pattern.

10. The fourth step in Monroe's motivated sequence pattern is visualization.

11. In the refutation organizational pattern, each main point addresses and then disproves an opposing claim.

MULTIPLE-CHOICE QUESTIONS

12. Which of these factors is important when considering organizational pattern?
    A) the nature of possible counterarguments
    B) the nature of the speech setting
    C) the nature of the specific speech purpose
    D) all of the above

13. A claim that addresses issues of judgment is called a
    A) judgment claim.
    B) claim of policy.
    C) claim of value.
    D) claim of fact.

14. Which organizational pattern addresses main points and then disproves opposing claims?
    A) problem-solution
    B) refutation
    C) cause-effect
    D) comparative advantage

15. The first step of Monroe's motivated sequence pattern is
    A) action.
    B) attention.
    C) need.
    D) satisfaction.

16. Which step in Monroe's motivated sequence pattern identifies the proposed solution?
    A) action
    B) attention
    C) need
    D) satisfaction

17. Which pattern arranges points to demonstrate how a particular set of circumstances leads to a specific result?
    A) problem-solution
    B) refutation
    C) cause-effect
    D) comparative advantage

18. Which pattern demonstrates how the speaker's points are more favorable than alternative positions?
    A) problem-solution
    B) refutation
    C) cause-effect
    D) comparative advantage

19. When audience members strongly disagree with the speaker's claims, they are a(n) ______ audience.
    A) counter
    B) apathetic
    C) hostile
    D) uninformed

FILL-IN-THE-BLANK QUESTIONS

20. The ______ organizational pattern demonstrates a problem and then offers a solution.

21. The ______ pattern of arrangement disproves opposing claims.

22. The ______ pattern is a five-step process for arousing attention and inspiring action.

23. In the motivated sequence pattern, the ______ step isolates and describes the issue to be addressed.

24. In the motivated sequence pattern, the ______ step identifies the solution.

25. In the motivated sequence pattern, the ______ step involves making a direct request to the audience.

ESSAY AND SHORT ANSWER QUESTIONS

26. Describe the three factors that are critical to consider when choosing an organizational pattern.
27. Discuss specific strategies a speaker could use with a hostile audience.
28. Discuss specific strategies a speaker could use with a sympathetic audience.
29. Discuss the importance of the specific speech purpose.
30. Describe the steps in Monroe's motivated sequence pattern.
31. Give an example of a speech that uses the comparative advantage arrangement.

ANSWER KEY FOR CHAPTER 26

1. True (p. 376)
2. False (p. 376)
3. True (p. 376)
4. False (p. 377)
5. True (p. 377)
6. False (p. 377)
7. True (p. 378)
8. False (p. 379)
9. False (pp. 380–383)
10. True (p. 382)
11. True (p. 384)
12. C (p. 376)
13. C (p. 376)
14. B (p. 384)
15. B (p. 380)
16. D (p. 381)
17. C (p. 385)
18. D (p. 385)
19. C (p. 377)
20. problem-solution (p. 385)
21. refutation (p. 385)
22. motivated sequence (p. 380)
23. need (p. 381)
24. satisfaction (p. 381)
25. action (p. 383)
26. (No answer, p. 376)
27. (No answer, p. 378)
28. (No answer, p. 378)
29. (No answer, p. 378)
30. (No answer, p. 382)
31. (No answer, p. 383)

Special Occasion Speeches 27

TRUE/FALSE QUESTIONS

1. The one underlying function of a special occasion speech is to entertain.
2. Special occasion speeches can be either informative or persuasive.
3. A commemorative special occasion speech is one that might occur at a wedding, anniversary, or retirement party.
4. Special occasion speeches may function to celebrate a person or event.
5. The goal of a speech of introduction is to inspire the audience.
6. A person who delivers a speech of introduction should not mention the speaker's awards, accomplishments, and achievements.
7. The final part of the introducer's task is to talk about herself or himself.
8. Speakers who have been introduced should respond to the introduction by briefly acknowledging and thanking the introducer.
9. Speakers who have been introduced should avoid using humor in response to the introduction.
10. The purpose of a speech of acceptance is to express gratitude for the honor bestowed on the speaker.
11. In a speech of acceptance, it is always appropriate for the speaker to say, "I really just don't know what to say."
12. The goals of a speech of presentation are to communicate the meaning of the award and to explain why the recipient is receiving it.
13. A roast is a brief tribute to a person or event being celebrated.
14. A verbal tribute to a deceased person is called a *eulogy.*
15. When delivering a eulogy, the speaker should focus on the life of the person rather than the circumstances of death.
16. In general, an after-dinner speech is expected to be somber and serious.

17. After-dinner speeches always take place after an evening meal.

18. A speaker should usually avoid presenting a stand-up comedy routine during an after-dinner speech.

19. The purpose of an after-dinner speech may be to entertain or set a social agenda.

20. A speech of inspiration attempts to uplift the audience and help them see things in a positive light.

21. Inspirational speeches are rarely used in the business world.

22. In a speech of inspiration, the speaker often uses pathos to appeal to the audience.

23. A speaker's positive ethos is critical to an effective inspirational speech.

24. Ethical inspirational speakers should not attempt to evoke emotion in their listeners.

25. A dynamic delivery style is inappropriate for a speech of inspiration.

26. A speaker's delivery style is not critical to the success of a special occasion speech.

27. In delivering an inspirational speech, the speaker should make the goal of the speech clear to the audience.

28. Inspirational speeches should be concluded with a dramatic ending.

29. Many successful inspirational speakers use acronyms as devices to organize their speeches.

MULTIPLE-CHOICE QUESTIONS

30. Which of the following is a function of a special occasion speech?
    A) to make a compelling argument
    B) to change an audience's beliefs
    C) to set a social agenda
    D) all of the above

31. Banquets, awards dinners, and roasts are examples of special occasion speeches that usually strive to
    A) commemorate.
    B) entertain.
    C) inspire.
    D) set a social agenda.

32. Fund-raisers, campaign banquets, conferences, and conventions are examples of special occasion speeches that strive to
    A) commemorate.
    B) entertain.
    C) inspire.
    D) set a social agenda.

33. Anniversaries of important events and memorial dedications are examples of special occasion speeches that strive to
   A) commemorate.
   B) entertain.
   C) inspire.
   D) set a social agenda.

34. A speaker who delivers a speech of introduction should avoid
   A) preparing for the speech.
   B) talking briefly.
   C) evaluating or offering critical commentary on the speech of the person being introduced.
   D) all of the above.

35. In a speech of introduction, the introducer's task is to tell the audience something about
   A) the speaker's shortcomings.
   B) the speaker's background.
   C) the speaker's attire.
   D) all of the above.

36. A speaker who has been introduced should respond to the introduction by
   A) acknowledging the introducer.
   B) thanking the introducer.
   C) using a combination of humility and humor.
   D) doing all of the above.

37. The function of a speech of acceptance is to
   A) express gratitude for the honor bestowed.
   B) react with surprise.
   C) question whether the speaker should have been given the award.
   D) describe the speaker's background and accomplishments.

38. For a speech of presentation, the speaker should
   A) assume the audience knows the meaning of the award.
   B) assume the audience knows why the recipient is receiving the award.
   C) plan the actual presentation of the award.
   D) do none of the above.

39. In a speech of presentation, the speaker should
   A) convey the meaning of the award.
   B) identify the sponsors of the award.
   C) explain why the recipient is being honored.
   D) do all of the above.

40. Several of Anne's closest friends celebrated their twenty-year friendship with her by delivering a series of short comical accounts of their relationship with Anne. Which type of special occasion speech did Anne's friends use?
   A) a toast
   B) a roast
   C) a eulogy
   D) an after-dinner speech

41. People with little or no public speaking experience will most likely deliver which type of special occasion speech at some point in their lives?
A) a toast
B) a roast
C) a eulogy
D) an after-dinner speech

42. When delivering a eulogy, the speaker should be sure to
A) avoid mentioning the deceased's family.
B) focus on the circumstances of the death.
C) show intense grief.
D) emphasize the deceased's positive qualities.

43. One of the most famous after-dinner speakers in U.S. history is
A) Mark Twain.
B) Abraham Lincoln.
C) Robert Frost.
D) Albert Einstein.

44. A speaker delivering an after-dinner speech may
A) attempt to entertain the audience.
B) choose social agenda-setting as his or her purpose.
C) find a topic that is engaging.
D) do all of the above.

45. The purpose of a speech of inspiration is
A) to uplift members of the audience
B) to change the opinion of the audience
C) to celebrate an event.
D) to do all of the above.

46. Examples of ordinary people who triumph over adversity and achieve extraordinary dreams are often used in a
A) speech of introduction.
B) speech of inspiration.
C) eulogy.
D) speech of acceptance.

47. One of the most successful strategies a speaker can use in inspirational speaking is
A) memorizing the speech.
B) using charts and graphs.
C) incorporating hypothetical examples.
D) employing a dynamic speaking style.

FILL-IN-THE-BLANK QUESTIONS

48. The function of a(n) _____ speech is to entertain, celebrate, commemorate, inspire, or set a social agenda.

49. Banquets, awards dinners, and roasts are examples of special occasion speeches that have as their purpose to _____.

50. A speech of ______ is a short speech that prepares the audience for another speaker and motivates them to listen.

51. In a speech of ______, the recipient expresses gratitude for the honor bestowed on him or her and acknowledges others who have contributed to his or her success.

52. In a speech of ______, the speaker communicates the importance of the award and explains why the recipient is receiving it.

53. A type of special occasion speech that is a brief tribute to a person or event being celebrated is referred to as a(n) ______.

54. A type of special occasion speech that is a humorous tribute to a person, one in which a series of speakers poke fun at him or her, is called a(n) ______.

55. A(n) ______ is a tribute to a deceased person.

56. A lighthearted and entertaining speech delivered before, during, or after a meal is called a(n) ______ speech.

57. A speech of ______ seeks to uplift the audience and help them see things in a positive light.

ESSAY AND SHORT ANSWER QUESTIONS

58. Provide tips for delivering an effective eulogy.

59. Explain how a speaker can deliver a successful speech of inspiration..

60. Discuss three functions of a speech of introduction.

61. How does a speech of acceptance differ from a speech of presentation?

62. Why is it important for a speech of introduction to be brief?

63. How can a speaker who has been introduced respond appropriately to the remarks made by the introducer?

64. List two tips for making a speech of acceptance.

65. What are the goals of a speech of presentation?

66. Explain the difference between a roast and a toast.

67. Name two things that a speaker should concentrate on when delivering a eulogy.

68. What is the general purpose of an after-dinner speech?

69. Give an example of a speech of inspiration.

70. Discuss which of the three classical persuasive appeals is most important when delivering an effective inspirational speech.

71. Give an example of using an acronym to organize an inspirational speech.

72. Why is the speaker's delivery style important in a speech of inspiration?

ANSWER KEY FOR CHAPTER 27

1. False (p. 393)
2. True (p. 393)
3. False (pp. 393–394)
4. True (p. 393)
5. False (p. 395)
6. False (p. 395)
7. False (p. 395)
8. True (p. 396)
9. False (p. 396)
10. True (p. 396)
11. False (p. 397)
12. True (p. 398)
13. False (p. 399)
14. True (p. 400)
15. True (p. 401)
16. False (p. 402)
17. False (p. 402)
18. True (p. 402)
19. True (pp. 402–403)
20. True (p. 403)
21. False (p. 403)
22. True (p. 403)
23. True (p. 404)
24. False (p. 405)
25. False (p. 404)
26. False (p. 404)
27. True (p. 404)
28. True (p. 405)
29. True (p. 404)
30. C (p. 393)
31. B (p. 393)
32. D (p. 394)
33. A (p. 394)
34. C (p. 395)
35. B (p. 395)
36. D (p. 396)
37. A (p. 396)
38. C (p. 399)
39. D (pp. 398–399)
40. B (p. 399)
41. C (p. 400)
42. D (p. 401)
43. A (p. 402)
44. D (pp. 402–403)
45. A (p. 403)
46. B (p. 403)
47. D (p. 404)
48. special occasion (p. 393)
49. entertain (p. 393)
50. introduction (p. 395)
51. acceptance (p. 396)
52. presentation (p. 398)
53. toast (p. 399)
54. roast (p. 399)
55. eulogy (p. 400)
56. after-dinner (p. 402)
57. inspiration (p. 403)
58. (No answer, p. 401)
59. (No answer, p. 404)
60. (No answer, p. 395)
61. (No answer, pp. 396–400)
62. (No answer, p. 395)
63. (No answer, p. 396)
64. (No answer, pp. 397–398)
65. (No answer, p. 398)
66. (No answer, p. 399)
67. (No answer, p. 400)
68. (No answer, p. 402)
69. (No answer, p. 403)
70. (No answer, pp. 403–404)
71. (No answer, p. 404)
72. (No answer, p. 404)

28 *Communicating in Groups*

TRUE/FALSE QUESTIONS

1. Group members' roles that are directly related to the accomplishment of the group's objectives and mission are called *interpersonal roles.*
2. There is no such thing as productive conflict.
3. Groupthink is the tendency of group participants to accept information and ideas only after critical evaluation and analysis.
4. Personal-based conflict is a form of unproductive conflict.
5. Issues-based conflict enhances effective decision making.
6. Counterproductive roles include "the blocker" and "the distractor."
7. Most negative experiences in groups result from the lack of a clear goal.
8. When member participation is unbalanced in groups, problems often arise and cause participants to be dissatisfied.
9. Effective group decision making is generally best accomplished through John Dewey's six-step process.
10. Before beginning to solve a problem, each group member should share his or her perception of what the problem is.
11. An agenda doesn't specify time limits for items of business.
12. A small group usually consists of three to twenty people.
13. As group members generate solutions, the merit of each idea should be evaluated and debated immediately.
14. John Dewey contended that his decision-making process encourages group members to "think reflectively" about their task.
15. Group presentations and individual presentations share very few characteristics.
16. In group presentations, task assignments are often linked to each member's task roles in the group.

MULTIPLE-CHOICE QUESTIONS

17. In a group setting, "the information giver," "the moderator," "the elaborator," and "the initiator" are examples of
    A) interpersonal roles.
    B) dyadic roles.
    C) task roles.
    D) counterproductive roles.

18. In a group setting, "the harmonizer," "the gatekeeper," and "the sensor" are examples of
    A) interpersonal roles.
    B) dyadic roles.
    C) task roles.
    D) counterproductive roles.

19. In a group setting, "the blocker," "the avoider," "the distracter," and "the dominator" are examples of
    A) interpersonal roles.
    B) dyadic roles.
    C) task roles.
    D) counterproductive roles.

20. Productive conflict is
    A) issues-based.
    B) personal-based.
    C) groupthink-based.
    D) motivation-based.

21. Groups prone to groupthink typically exhibit which of the following behaviors?
    A) Participants reach a consensus unwillingly, often because they don't genuinely agree with each other.
    B) Members who do not agree with the majority of the group are not pressured to conform.
    C) Disagreement, difficult questions, and counterproposals are encouraged.
    D) More group effort is spent testing the decision than rationalizing or justifying it.

22. Directly asking members to contribute, redirecting the discussion, and setting a positive tone are three techniques that group leaders can use to encourage
    A) participation.
    B) groupthink.
    C) friendship.
    D) status differences.

23. The first three steps in Dewey's group decision-making process are
    A) identify the problem, establish guidelines and criteria, generate solutions.
    B) identify the problem, generate solutions, conduct research and analysis.
    C) identify the problem, generate solutions, select the best solution.
    D) identify the problem, conduct research and analysis, establish guidelines and criteria.

24. The final three steps in Dewey's group decision-making process are
    A) evaluate solutions, conduct research and analysis, select the best solution.
    B) establish guidelines and criteria, evaluate solutions, conduct research and analysis.
    C) generate solutions, select the best solution, evaluate solutions.
    D) generate solutions, evaluate solutions, select the best solution.

25. Arguing for the sake of raising concerns about an idea is called
    A) groupthink.
    B) devil's advocacy.
    C) an agenda.
    D) interpersonal responsibility.

26. When preparing for a group presentation, members should
    A) assign more difficult tasks to the more intelligent group members.
    B) select two or three moderators.
    C) aim for consistency in delivery styles.
    D) do all of the above.

FILL-IN-THE-BLANK QUESTIONS

27. Group members' relational roles that facilitate group interaction are called ______ roles.

28. Group members' roles that are directly related to the accomplishment of the group's objectives and mission are called ______ roles.

29. A type of conflict in which questions are clarified, ideas are challenged, counterexamples are presented, worst-case scenarios are considered, and proposals are reformulated is called ______ conflict.

30. ______ conflict is a destructive form of conflict in which members argue about one another instead of with one another.

31. ______ is the tendency of group participants to accept information and ideas without critical evaluation and analysis.

32. ______ conflict is a type of productive conflict that allows members to test and debate ideas and potential solutions.

33. Negative or ______ roles include "the blocker" and "the avoider."

34. As group members generate ______, the merit of each idea should not be evaluated and debated.

35. In group presentations, task assignments are often linked to each member's task ______ in the group.

ESSAY AND SHORT ANSWER QUESTIONS

36. List three ways to promote productive conflict among group members.

37. Describe three methods that you could use as a group member to discourage groupthink.

38. Explain the difference between personal-based conflict and issues-based conflict.

39. Why are both interpersonal roles and task roles important to effective group decision making?

40. List and describe two counterproductive group roles.

41. Explain the steps in Dewey's decision-making process.

42. Compare and contrast two characteristics of group presentations and individual presentations.

43. List two guidelines for preparing team presentations.

ANSWER KEY FOR CHAPTER 28

1. False (pp. 421–422)
2. False (p. 423)
3. False (p. 423)
4. True (p. 423)
5. True (p. 423)
6. True (p. 423)
7. True (p. 424)
8. True (p. 425)
9. True (p. 426)
10. True (p. 426)
11. False (p. 421)
12. True (p. 421)
13. False (p. 426)
14. True (p. 426)
15. False (p. 426)
16. True (p. 427)
17. C (pp. 421–422)
18. A (p. 422)
19. D (pp. 422–423)
20. A (p. 423)
21. A (p. 423)
22. A (p. 425)
23. D (p. 426)
24. C (p. 426)
25. B (p. 423)
26. C (p. 428)
27. interpersonal (p. 422)
28. task (pp. 421–422)
29. productive (p. 423)
30. Personal-based (p. 423)
31. Groupthink (p. 423)
32. Issues-based (p. 423)
33. counterproductive (pp. 422–423)
34. solutions (p. 426)
35. role (p. 427)
36. (No answer, p. 423)
37. (No answer, pp. 423–424)
38. (No answer, p. 423)
39. (No answer, pp. 421–422)
40. (No answer, p. 422)
41. (No answer, p. 426)
42. (No answer, pp. 426–427)
43. (No answer, p. 428)

Business and Professional Presentations 29

TRUE/FALSE QUESTIONS

1. Presentational speaking is generally less formal than public speaking.
2. Presentational speaking usually occurs in more limited settings than does public speaking.
3. Topics for business presentations are ordinarily chosen by the speaker.
4. Audiences often consider presentational speakers to have more expertise than public speakers.
5. In business and professional presentations, verbal interaction between speaker and audience is generally the rule rather than the exception.
6. A proposal is a presentation that gives detailed information about a procedure or device.
7. Monroe's motivated sequence offers an excellent way to organize sales presentations.
8. A staff report updates clients on developments in an ongoing market.
9. A sales presentation attempts to lead a potential buyer to purchase a service or a product described by the presenter.
10. A staff report is the same as a sales presentation.
11. A progress report is similar to a staff report.
12. The purpose of a crisis-response presentation is to reassure an organization's various audiences, not to restore credibility.
13. There are no set patterns of organization for a progress report.
14. Crisis-response presentations target only one audience.
15. To counteract problems in being understood, inexperienced ESL speakers should learn the presentation almost by heart.

MULTIPLE-CHOICE QUESTIONS

16. Presentational speaking takes which of the following forms?
    A) reports delivered by individuals or groups in a professional or business environment
    B) individual speakers addressing a group of colleagues, managers, clients, or customers
    C) multiple members of a work group addressing a similarly composed audience
    D) all of the above

17. Which of the following factors distinguish presentational speaking from public speaking?
    A) audience size, composition, and participation
    B) speaker appearance and professionalism
    C) counteractive duality
    D) all of the above

18. Sales presentations, proposals, progress reports, staff reports, and crisis-response presentations are examples of
    A) public speaking.
    B) presentational speaking.
    C) conversational speaking.
    D) ethical speaking.

19. Will gave a presentation that attempted to convince stockholders to purchase the new software he had developed. What type of presentation did Will give?
    A) a technical report
    B) a staff report
    C) a sales presentation
    D) a progress report

20. Dr. Buchanan informed her colleagues about the various intercom systems she had investigated. She then recommended that the university purchase a particular system. What type of presentation did Professor Buchanan give?
    A) a proposal
    B) a staff report
    C) a sales presentation
    D) a progress report

FILL-IN-THE-BLANK QUESTIONS

21. Reports delivered by individuals or groups within the business or professional environment take the form of ______ speaking.

22. ______ speaking is generally less formal than public speaking.

23. A(n) ______ presentation attempts to lead a potential buyer to purchase a service or product described by the presenter.

24. A(n) ______ is a presentation that gives detailed information about a procedure or device.

25. Alan Monroe's ______ offers an excellent way to organize sales presentations.

26. A(n) ______ report informs managers and employees of new work-related developments.

27. A(n) ______ report updates clients or principals on developments in an ongoing project.

ESSAY AND SHORT ANSWER QUESTIONS

28. How does public speaking differ from presentational speaking?

29. Why is there generally more verbal interaction between speaker and audience in a professional presentation than in a public speaking presentation?

30. Why is Monroe's motivated sequence effective for organizing sales presentations?

31. Describe the difference between a proposal and a staff report.

32. Discuss the elements of a crisis-response presentation.

ANSWER KEY FOR CHAPTER 29

1. True (p. 430)
2. True (p. 430)
3. False (p. 431)
4. False (p. 431)
5. True (p. 431)
6. True (p. 433)
7. True (p. 432)
8. False (p. 435)
9. True (p. 432)
10. False (p. 434)
11. True (p. 435)
12. False (p. 436)
13. True (p. 436)
14. False (p. 436)
15. True (p. 437)
16. D (p. 430)
17. A (p. 430)
18. B (p. 431)
19. C (p. 432)
20. A (p. 433)
21. presentational (p. 430)
22. Presentational (p. 430)
23. sales (p. 432)
24. proposal (p. 433)
25. motivated sequence (p. 432)
26. staff (p. 434)
27. progress (p. 435)
28. (No answer, p. 430)
29. (No answer, p. 431)
30. (No answer, pp. 432–433)
31. (No answer, pp. 433–434)
32. (No answer, pp. 436–437)

Speaking in Other College Courses 30

TRUE/FALSE QUESTIONS

1. After completing the introductory public speaking course, students will not usually be expected to speak publicly at college.

2. A panel discussion is an oral presentation prepared and delivered by a group of three or more individuals.

3. A poster session presents information about a study or an issue concisely and visually.

4. A debate is a type of oral presentation format in which two individuals or groups argue the issue in question from opposing viewpoints.

5. In preparing a poster session presentation, the speaker should use a standard-size poster board.

6. An amateur or outsider audience is a group of people who possess intimate knowledge of the topic or idea being discussed.

7. When presenting to an audience of colleagues within the field, it is safe to assume the audience shares knowledge of the general field under question.

8. The lay audience has the least amount of knowledge of the given field and topic.

9. Speakers addressing mixed audiences should prepare both detailed and general content.

10. Oral presentations in the sciences and mathematics often focus on describing the results of original or replicated research.

11. When presenting to a mixed audience, the speaker should consider devoting half to two-thirds of the presentation time on the introduction.

12. A methods/procedure presentation explains how an experimental or mathematical process works.

13. The purpose of the research overview presentation is to provide context and background for a research question or hypothesis that will form the basis of an impending study.

14. The research overview should ignore the weaknesses of research and focus only on the strengths.

15. The extended research or field study presentation should include a time line indicating how the results will be used in the future.

16. In many science and mathematical presentations, audience members will expect experimental evidence and mathematical proofs.

17. Scientific and statistical information is not made more comprehensible by illustrating it visually.

18. Oral presentations in technical courses often relate to a current project rather than to prior research.

19. In the request for funding a presentation, a member or team provides evidence that a project, proposal, or design is worth funding.

20. The request for funding a presentation usually begins with a list of specific reasons a particular project or idea should be funded.

21. Social scientists conduct qualitative as well as quantitative research.

22. A social science presentation often answers the *what, how*, and *why* questions.

23. The types of presentations delivered in science courses are different from presentations delivered in social science courses.

24. When social science students participate in a debate, they are never asked to advocate a position that they do not support.

25. The explanatory research presentation reports on studies that attempt to analyze and explain a phenomenon.

26. Social scientists never measure the effectiveness of programs developed to address social issues.

27. The review of the literature presentation reviews the body of research related to a given topic and offers conclusions about the topic based on this research.

28. In a policy recommendation presentation, the audience is a lay audience whose members usually have a vested interest in the problem but are unfamiliar with the intricacies of the field.

29. An effective social science presentation must make use of timely data.

30. Speaking assignments in the arts and humanities often require the speaker to interpret the meaning of a particular idea, event, person, story, or artifact.

31. Oral presentations in the arts and humanities include informative speeches of explanation, classroom discussions, and debates.

32. Types of presentations for the arts and humanities most commonly include lectures and group activities.

33. The most common and practical speaking event for education courses is classroom teaching.

34. A lecture is an informational speech for an audience of new student learners.

35. The classroom discussion presentation is intended as a short introduction to a group activity that follows a primary lecture.

36. Effective presentations in education require careful attention to the selection of a speech organizational pattern.

37. Successful oral presentations in education make use of examples and evidence with which the audience is familiar and can grasp.

38. A community service learning project report recommends the adoption of a new treatment or policy.

39. A shift report is a concise report of the patient's status and needs.

MULTIPLE-CHOICE QUESTIONS

40. College students may be asked to deliver oral presentations in the form of
    A) panel discussions.
    B) team presentations and debates.
    C) poster sessions.
    D) all of the above.

41. Which of the following types of audience is made up of people who possess intimate knowledge of the topic being discussed?
    A) expert
    B) colleagues within the field
    C) lay audience
    D) mixed audience

42. Which of the following types of audience might comprise academic co-workers, managers, project coordinators, or team leaders?
    A) expert
    B) colleagues within the field
    C) lay audience
    D) mixed audience

43. Which of the following types of audience brings to the presentation the least amount of knowledge of the given topic and field?
    A) expert
    B) colleagues within the field
    C) lay audience
    D) mixed audience

44. Which of the following types of audience consists of people who have expert knowledge along with those who have no specialized knowledge?
A) expert
B) colleagues within the field
C) lay audience
D) mixed audience

45. Science courses include those related to which sciences?
A) physical
B) natural
C) earth
D) all of the above

46. The ______ presentation for science and math describes original research that the speaker has conducted.
A) research
B) field study
C) research overview
D) all of the above

47. Which presentation format is designed to best convey technical, scientific, and social scientific information?
A) panel discussion
B) debate
C) poster session
D) all of the above

48. The purpose of the ______ presentation is to provide content and background for a research question or hypothesis.
A) research
B) field study
C) research overview
D) methods/procedure

49. In which presentations do audience members usually expect experimental evidence and statistical proofs?
A) science and math
B) social science
C) arts and humanities
D) education

50. The focus of ______ presentations is often a project the speaker is working on.
A) science and math
B) social science
C) technical
D) education

51. Which type of presentation provides evidence that a project, proposal, or design idea is worthy of financial support?
A) design review
B) technical
C) request for funding
D) policy recommendation

52. Effective presentations in the technical disciplines are
A) detailed and specific in the use of experimental results.
B) detailed and specific in the use of numbers.
C) detailed and specific in the use of evidence.
D) all of the above.

53. Which type of presentation measures the effectiveness of programs?
A) explanatory research
B) evaluation research
C) review of the literature
D) policy recommendation

54. Which type of presentation offers advice and suggestions on a current issue or problem?
A) explanatory research
B) evaluation research
C) review of the literature
D) policy recommendation

55. In the arts and humanities, an informative speech of explanation
A) would never discuss a school of philosophical thought.
B) always focuses on historical events.
C) might explain a piece of literature, art, or music.
D) usually deals with political leaders.

56. Effective presentations in the arts and humanities help the audience to think of the topic in a new way by providing a(n) ______ of/on the topic.
A) overview
B) debate
C) interpretation
D) all of the above

57. Sample presentations for education courses include
A) lectures.
B) group activities.
C) classroom discussions.
D) all of the above.

58. An effective presentation in education should
A) always have logical organization.
B) separate presentation content and overall course content.
C) ignore audience-relevant examples, evidence, and support.
D) always have chronological organization.

59. The ______ presentation teaches an audience about the need or problem in a community agency.
A) policy recommendation report
B) shift report
C) case conference
D) community service learning project

60. An approach to treatment in which caregivers make decisions based on current research and "best practices" is a(n)
A) policy recommendation report
B) evidence-based practice
C) shift report
D) case conference

FILL-IN-THE-BLANK QUESTIONS

61. A(n) ______ is an oral presentation prepared and delivered by a group of three or more individuals.

62. A(n) ______ presents information about a study or an issue concisely and visually for participants at professional conferences.

63. A(n) ______ is a type of oral presentation format in which two individuals or groups argue the issue in question from opposing viewpoints.

64. A group of people who possess intimate knowledge of the topic or idea being discussed are referred to as the ______ or insider audience.

65. A ______ audience is one that is unfamiliar with the topic.

66. Speakers addressing ______ audiences should prepare both detailed and general content.

67. Oral presentations in the ______ often focus on describing the results of original or replicated research.

68. A geology student reporting on a dig is an example of an extended research or ______ presentation.

69. The purpose of the ______ presentation is to provide context and background for a research question or hypothesis that will form the basis of an impending study.

70. In the ______ presentation, a member or team provides evidence that a project, proposal, or design is worth funding.

71. ______ scientists conduct qualitative research as well as quantitative research.

72. The ______ presentation reports on studies that attempt to analyze and explain a phenomenon.

73. The ______ presentation reviews the body of research related to a given topic and offers conclusions about the topic based on this research.

74. In a(n) ______ presentation, the audience is a lay audience whose members have a vested interest in the problem but are unfamiliar with the intricacies of the field.

75. Speaking assignments in the ______ often require the speaker to interpret the meaning of a particular idea, event, person, story, or artifact.

76. Types of presentations for ______ include lectures and group activities.

77. A(n) ______ is a concise report of the patient's status and needs given to the oncoming caregiver.

78. The ______ presentation recommends the adoption of a new treatment or policy.

ESSAY AND SHORT ANSWER QUESTIONS

79. Identify three necessary components of an oral review of an academic article.

80. Compare and contrast the characteristics of team presentations, panel discussions, and poster sessions.

81. Give the characteristics of two types of typical audiences.
82. What is the difference between the expert audience and colleagues within the field?
83. How does a lay audience differ from a mixed audience?
84. List three tips for presenting information to a mixed audience.
85. How can a speaker effectively evaluate his or her original research presentation?
86. List three tips for producing an effective poster session.
87. List three tips for preparing a successful scientific presentation.
88. Name two types of technical presentations.
89. Identify two characteristics of an effective technical presentation.
90. Explain the differences between qualitative and quantitative research.
91. Name two types of social science presentations.
92. Identify two characteristics of an effective social science presentation.
93. Name two types of arts and humanities presentations.
94. Identify two characteristics of an effective arts and humanities presentation.
95. Name two types of education presentations.
96. Identify two characteristics of an effective education presentation.
97. Explain the parts of a community service learning project.
98. Name the types of nursing and allied health presentations.
99. Explain how to give an effective nursing and allied health presentation.

ANSWER KEY FOR CHAPTER 30

1. False (p. 439)
2. False (p. 440)
3. True (p. 440)
4. True (p. 440)
5. True (p. 444)
6. False (p. 440)
7. False (p. 440)
8. True (p. 440)
9. True (p. 440)
10. True (pp. 440–441)
11. True (p. 441)
12. True (p. 442)
13. True (p. 443)
14. False (p. 443)
15. True (p. 444)
16. True (p. 444)
17. False (pp. 445–446)
18. True (p. 445)
19. True (p. 446)
20. False (p. 446)
21. True (p. 447)
22. True (p. 447)
23. False (p. 447)
24. False (p. 447)
25. True (p. 448)
26. False (p. 448)
27. True (p. 448)
28. True (p. 449)
29. True (p. 449)
30. True (p. 449)
31. True (p. 449)
32. False (pp. 451–452)
33. True (p. 451)
34. True (p. 451)
35. False (p. 452)
36. True (p. 452)
37. True (p. 453)
38. False (p. 453)
39. True (p. 454)
40. D (pp. 439–440)
41. A (p. 440)
42. B (p. 440)
43. C (p. 440)
44. D (p. 440)
45. D (p. 440)
46. A (p. 441)
47. C (p. 443)
48. C (p. 443)
49. A (p. 444)
50. C (p. 445)
51. C (p. 446)
52. D (p. 447)
53. B (p. 448)
54. D (p. 449)
55. C (p. 449)
56. C (p. 449)
57. D (pp. 451–452)
58. A (p. 452)
59. D (p. 453)
60. B (p. 453)
61. team presentation (p. 440)
62. poster session (p. 440)
63. debate (p. 440)
64. expert (p. 440)
65. lay (p. 440)
66. mixed (p. 441)
67. sciences and math (pp. 440–441)
68. field study (p. 443)
69. research overview (p. 443)
70. request for funding (p. 446)
71. Social (p. 447)
72. explanatory research (p. 448)
73. review of literature (p. 448)
74. policy recommendation (p. 449)
75. arts and humanities (p. 449)
76. education (p. 451)
77. shift report (p. 454)
78. policy recommendation report (p. 454)
79. (No answer, p. 439)
80. (No answer, pp. 440)
81. (No answer, p. 440)
82. (No answer, p. 440)
83. (No answer, p. 440)
84. (No answer, p. 441)
85. (No answer, p. 442)
86. (No answer, p. 443)
87. (No answer, p. 445)
88. (No answer, p. 446)
89. (No answer, pp. 446–447)
90. (No answer, p. 447)
91. (No answer, pp. 447–449)
92. (No answer, p. 449)
93. (No answer, p. 450)
94. (No answer, pp. 450–451)
95. (No answer, pp. 451–453)
96. (No answer, pp. 452–453)
97. (No answer, p. 453)
98. (No answer, pp. 453–454)
99. (No answer, p. 454)

ANSWER KEY FOR COMPREHENSIVE FINAL EXAM

1. B (pp. 7–8) Ch. 1
2. C (p. 9) Ch. 1
3. D (p. 14) Ch. 1
4. B (p. 18) Ch. 2
5. B (p. 19) Ch. 2
6. D (p. 19) Ch. 2
7. A (p. 38) Ch. 3
8. B (p. 45) Ch. 3
9. D (p. 45) Ch. 3
10. C (p. 49) Ch. 4
11. B (p. 55) Ch. 4
12. C (p. 52) Ch. 4
13. C (p. 63) Ch. 5
14. B (pp. 66–71) Ch. 5
15. B (p. 67) Ch. 5
16. D (pp. 78–79) Ch. 6
17. B (p. 79) Ch. 6
18. C (p. 82) Ch. 6
19. A (p. 95) Ch. 7
20. A (p. 95) Ch. 7
21. D (p. 118) Ch. 8
22. D (pp. 116–117) Ch. 8
23. A (p. 116) Ch. 8
24. B (p. 118) Ch. 8
25. C (p. 130) Ch. 9
26. B (p. 139) Ch. 9
27. A (p. 138) Ch. 9
28. A (p. 153) Ch. 10
29. D (p. 157) Ch. 10
30. B (p. 154) Ch. 10
31. B (p. 174) Ch. 11
32. D (p. 180) Ch. 11
33. B (p. 182) Ch. 11
34. A (p. 185) Ch. 12
35. B (p. 185) Ch. 12
36. C (p. 185) Ch. 12
37. A (p. 192) Ch. 13
38. C (p. 194) Ch. 13
39. A (p. 216) Ch. 14
40. A (p. 215) Ch. 14
41. C (p. 222) Ch. 14
42. C (p. 223) Ch. 15
43. A (p. 224) Ch. 15
44. C (p. 227) Ch. 15
45. A (p. 230) Ch. 16
46. A (p. 234) Ch. 16
47. B (p. 237) Ch. 16
48. C (p. 252) Ch. 17
49. B (p. 253) Ch. 17
50. C (p. 256) Ch. 17
51. D (p. 261) Ch. 18
52. A (p. 264) Ch. 18
53. D (p. 265) Ch. 18
54. A (p. 269) Ch. 19
55. A (p. 272) Ch. 19
56. D (p. 275) Ch. 19
57. C (p. 282) Ch. 20
58. A (p. 288) Ch. 20
59. C (p. 288) Ch. 20
60. A (p. 295) Ch. 21
61. A (p. 295) Ch. 21
62. D (p. 298) Ch. 21
63. B (p. 304) Ch. 22
64. C (p. 309) Ch. 22
65. C (p. 306) Ch. 22
66. C (p. 327) Ch. 23
67. A (p. 333) Ch. 23
68. C (p. 331) Ch. 23
69. D (p. 346) Ch. 24
70. C (p. 351) Ch. 24
71. B (p. 361) Ch. 25
72. B (p. 368) Ch. 25
73. A (pp. 373–374) Ch. 25
74. D (p. 383) Ch. 26
75. A (p. 376) Ch. 26
76. C (p. 394) Ch. 27
77. C (p. 395) Ch. 27
78. D (p. 404) Ch. 27
79. D (p. 422) Ch. 28
80. A (p. 423) Ch. 28
81. A (p. 423) Ch. 28
82. D (p. 430) Ch. 29
83. A (p. 433) Ch. 29
84. C (p. 443) Ch. 30
85. B (p. 440) Ch. 30
86. C (p. 440) Ch. 30
87. A (p. 452) Ch. 30

DISCUSSION QUESTIONS

1. What is the general purpose of this speech? What is the specific purpose? What is the thesis?

   The general purpose of the Reverend Tom Grey's speech is to persuade; the specific purpose is to persuade the U.S. House Judiciary Committee to enact H.R. 497. The thesis, or his claim, in this persuasive speech is that "the expansion of gambling is bad for families and businesses."

2. How would you describe Grey's credibility? How would you describe the credibility of the arguments he presents?

   First, his position as executive director of the National Coalition against Legalized Gambling establishes his credibility with respect to his ability to speak on the subject of gambling. In addition, the speaker establishes his own credibility when he talks about his travels during the last three years, during which he talked to countless thousands of Americans. Finally, Grey establishes his credibility and the credibility of his arguments by referring to objective, academic studies and recounting the results of referenda on legalized gambling in numerous states.

3. Did Grey adequately gain his audience's attention in the introduction of this speech?

   He gains the audience's attention by characterizing legalized gambling as a battle between well-funded gambling promoters with hidden political agendas and ordinary citizens trying to protect their communities. He uses visual language to characterize and exaggerate the characteristics of the bad guys—the gambling promoters.

4. What type of claim (fact, value, policy) does the speaker argue?

   The speaker's claim that H.R. 497 should be passed is a policy claim. Recall that speakers use claims of policy when recommending that a specific course of action be taken or approved of by an audience. As is common with claims of policy, Grey's argument also involves claims of fact and claims of value. His claims of fact involve focusing on the effects of gambling, and his claim of value is that legalized gambling is bad. This is a judgment, even though Grey denies that it is a moral judgment.

5. Do you think there are any logical fallacies in Grey's reasoning and arguments?

   Bandwagoning and overgeneralization are two of the possible areas that one might argue are fallacious in Grey's reasoning. First, with bandwagoning, the speaker assigns a claim greater substance by making it appear more popular than it really is. This speaker asserts that voters from every walk of life recognize that gambling is poor public policy. Apparently this is not true in all states, for all voters, or for all types of gambling, as many constituents are voting for particular types of gambling. For instance, Grey notes that Virginians opposed casinos on riverboats; however, he fails to note that Virginians previously voted for a state lottery but voted down a racetrack in Hampton Roads. In terms of overgeneralization, where a speaker asserts that a particular piece of evidence is true for everyone concerned, Grey claims that gambling is bad for families and businesses. Perhaps he did not survey residents or business owners in Las Vegas or Atlantic City, where casino expansion creates many jobs and generates tourism, which infuses the community with capital from outside sources.

Live Longer and Healthier: Stop Eating Meat! by Renzi Stone

While he was a student at the University of Oklahoma, Renzi Stone delivered this persuasive speech to his public speaking class. The speech is noteworthy because of its strong, attention-grabbing introduction. To persuade his audience to listen to his claims about the benefits of vegetarianism, Stone first refutes several stereotypes about vegetarians. Why do you think he starts the speech this way? How convincing are his arguments in support of vegetarianism?

What do Steve Martin, Dustin Hoffman, Albert Einstein, Jerry Garcia, Michael Stipe, Eddie Vedder, Martina Navratilova, Carl Lewis, and 12 million other Americans all have in common? All of these well-known people were or are vegetarians. What do they know that we don't? Consuming a regimen of high-fat, high-protein flesh foods is a sure-fire prescription for disaster, like running diesel fuel through your car's gasoline engine. In the book, *Why Do Vegetarians Eat Like That?*, David Gabbe asserts that millions of people today are afflicted with chronic diseases that can be directly linked to the consumption of meat. Eating a vegetarian diet can help prevent many of those diseases.

In 1996, 12 million Americans identified themselves as vegetarians. That number is twice as many as in the decade before. According to a recent National Restaurant Association poll found in *Health* magazine, one in five diners say they now go out of their way to choose restaurants that serve at least a few meatless entrees. Obviously, the traditionally American trait of a meat-dominated society has subsided in recent years.

In discussing vegetarianism today, first I will tell how vegetarians are perceived in society. Next, I will introduce several studies validating my claim that a meatless diet is extraordinarily healthy. I will then show how a veggie diet can strengthen the immune system and make the meatless body a shield from unwanted diseases such as cancer and heart disease. Maintaining a strict vegetarian diet can also lead to a longer life. Finally, I will put an image into the audiences' mind of a meatless society that relies on vegetables for the main course at breakfast, lunch, and dinner.

Moving to my first point, society generally holds two major misperceptions about vegetarians. First of all, society often perceives vegetarians as a radical group of people with extreme principles. In this view, vegetarians are seen as a monolithic group of people who choose to eat vegetables because they are opposed to the killing of animals for food. The second major misconception is that because vegetarians do not eat meat, they do not get the proper amounts of essential vitamins and minerals often found in meat.

Here is my response to these misconceived notions. First of all, vegetarians are not a homogeneous group of radicals. Whereas many vegetarians in the past did join the movement on the principle that killing animals is wrong, many join the movement today mainly for its health benefits. In addition, there are many different levels of vegetarianism. Some vegetarians eat nothing but vegetables. Others don't eat red meat, but do occasionally eat chicken and fish.

Secondly, contrary to popular opinion, vegetarians get more than enough vitamins and minerals in their diet and generally receive healthier nourishment than meat eaters. In fact, in an article for *Health* magazine, Peter Jaret states that vegetarians actually get larger amounts of amino acids due to the elimination of saturated fats, which are often found in meat products. Studies show that the health benefits of a veggie lifestyle contribute to increased life expectancy and overall productivity.

Hopefully you now see that society's perceptions of vegetarians are outdated and just plain wrong. You are familiar with many of the problems associated with a meat-based diet, and you have heard many of the benefits of a vegetarian diet. Now try to imagine how you personally can improve your life by becoming a vegetarian.

Can you imagine a world where people retire at age 80 and lead productive lives into their early 100s? Close your eyes and think about celebrating your 70th wedding anniversary, seeing your great-grandchildren get married, and witnessing 100 years of world events and technological innovations. David Gabbe's book refers to studies that have shown a vegetarian diet can increase your life expectancy up to 15 years. A longer life is within your reach, and the diet you eat has a direct impact on your health and how you age.

In conclusion, vegetarianism is a healthy life choice, not a radical cult. By eliminating meat from their diets, vegetarians reap the benefits of a vegetable-based diet that helps prevent disease and increase life expectancy. People, take heed of my advice. There are many more sources of information available for those who want to take a few hours to research the benefits of the veggie lifestyle. If you don't believe my comments, discover the whole truth for yourself.

Twelve million Americans know the health benefits that come with being a vegetarian. Changing your eating habits can be just as easy as making your bed in the morning. Sure it takes a few extra minutes and some thought, but your body will thank you in the long run.

You only live once. Why not make it a long stay?

DISCUSSION QUESTIONS

1. What is the general purpose of this speech? What is its specific purpose?

   The general purpose of this speech is to persuade; the specific purpose is to persuade the audience to become informed about the benefits of becoming a vegetarian.

2. What persuasive model can best be applied to Renzi Stone's speech?

   Monroe's motivated sequence is the model that this speech is based on. First, the speaker establishes a need for improving the perception of vegetarianism. Then he offers the health benefits of vegetarianism as a means of satisfying this need.

3. What are the two main ideas that Stone uses to establish a need for improving the image of vegetarians?

   His first idea is that the general public believes that you don't get minimum amounts of essential vitamins and minerals without consuming meat. The second point Stone offers to establish need is the idea that the vegetarian lifestyle is too inclusive—that it is an all-or-nothing venture based on principle rather than on health needs.

4. In the satisfaction stage of the sequence, what does Stone argue?

   He argues that vegetarians get more than enough vitamins and minerals and better amino acids. Second, he argues that there are many different types of vegetarianism to accommodate all levels of interest.

5. Describe the visual imagery Stone uses to drive his point home.

   Stone has his listeners imagine what their future will be like, how much longer they will live, and how much they will enjoy spending that time with their families.

6. What specific action does Stone request of his audience?

   He simply asks that people take a few hours to access sources of information and to seriously consider changing to vegetarianism based on the benefits noted in the research.

Making Dreams Reality by Amber Mixon

Amber Mixon delivered this informative speech to her public speaking class at the University of Oklahoma. Note how Mixon effectively introduces her speech topic by asking her classmates to think about world hunger in terms of how much money a typical college student spends on food each day. She goes on to clearly explain how an organization called Feed the Children is addressing world hunger and related problems, and how students can volunteer their time and energy to support this cause.

Did you know that 20 percent of children in the United States under eighteen years of age are hungry? Consider for a moment the amount of money that you as a college student spend in a single day on food alone. Did you know that 1.3 billion people worldwide live on less than one dollar a day? Have you ever volunteered your time to help the hungry? When some students think of volunteering, they focus on the benefits that it brings to their standing in a school organization or the status it earns them on their résumé rather than thinking about how important it is to help those less fortunate than they are.

However, even if people choose to ignore the hunger problem in our world, one organization has dared to bridge the gap between the impoverished and those unaware of these circumstances. That organization is Feed the Children. Though I don't volunteer often, I have been lucky enough to experience the fulfillment FTC workers experi-